T0107967

Contents

Foreword

Thank you for picking up this book.

I would like to start by offering you this phrase: *Tohosenshu*, *zaihoshojo*, *fukujuzocho*. Roughly translated, this means, "May all crimes or disasters disappear from the lives of all living things, and may they experience good fortune." It appears at the beginning of a sutra that is chanted before every meal, and gives us a small insight into why, in Japanese culture, we always put our hands together before and after every meal.

Shojin ryori ("divine cuisine") or Zen vegan food, the traditional Buddhist cuisine that has evolved over centuries in Japan, is often thought of as being restricted to traditional Japanese dishes. I hope you'll be pleasantly surprised to find that many of the recipes in this book don't look like temple food at all.

Personally, I am someone who likes to challenge my own assumptions. Our state of mind and our attitude can have a great effect on how we perceive the events of daily life. If we can adopt an open-minded attitude when it comes to food, we may find that we come to like something that we previously avoided.

Even the most unconventional recipes in this book pay respect to tradition and history, and as far as possible use every part of each ingredient. I have done my best to make the recipes easy to prepare in home kitchens. If this book can show you how interesting Zen vegan cooking can be, and help you become more familiar with Buddhism, I will be truly grateful. I hope you enjoy this book.

Gassho,
Koyu Iinuma

Zen Vegan Basics

What is Zen vegan food?

The Zen vegan food in this book is based on traditional *shojin ryori* Buddhist temple cuisine, which is made without any meat, utilizing vegetables, beans and grains. Buddhist monks in training, who are forbidden from killing any being, eat this kind of food every day so as to not take life from any living creature.

Zen vegan food is prepared with care

Buddhism was started by Buddha, or Shakyamuni, about 2,500 years ago. It is said that Buddha spread the way of Buddhism by tailoring his message according to the way of thinking and position of each person that he preached his philosophies to. This was based on the principle of *chudo*, which means taking the middle road, never straying too far to one side or another, and accepting all kinds of people.

In Zen vegan cuisine, the balance between the five flavors—sour, bitter, sweet, hot (spicy) and salty—is very important. In particular, the *tanmi*, or subtle flavors inherent in the ingredients, are highly prized. Flavors in a dish need to be balanced carefully to bring out the full taste of each ingredient. The "tan" of *tanmi*, which means "not heavy," corresponds to the middle road espoused by the Buddha. The "middle road" can be applied to cooking by creating food that has the perfect balance. This balance varies from person to person: some prefer food that is spicier, while others prefer sweeter-tasting dishes. It is important in Zen vegan cooking to always think of the preferences of the diner, to adjust the flavor balance to their liking to make them happy, and to work with care and attention to detail—in other words, to show your care for other people.

The Basic Rules of Zen Buddhist Temple Cooking

All the recipes in this book follow the rules below. They may seem daunting at first glance, but they are no obstacle to creating a wide range of delicious Zen vegan dishes.

No animal-based proteins are used

In traditional Buddhist temple cuisine, animal-based ingredients are prohibited because of the Buddhist commandment that forbids the killing of any living thing. Throughout Japanese history, several emperors who sought to encourage Buddhism issued edicts prohibiting the consumption of meat. A traditional Buddhist diet uses soybean products, particularly tofu, as the main source of protein.

Dashi stock must be vegan

Dashi stock is the foundation of conventional traditional Japanese cuisine. In Zen vegan cooking, however, dashi stock cannot be made with *katsuobushi* (flakes of dried bonito), *niboshi* (dried sardines) or any other animal products. In their stead, umami-rich vegetables such as dried kombu seaweed and shiitake mushrooms are used, as well as roasted soybeans and the soaking liquid from *kanpyo* (dried gourd strips). I especially recommend using the water that has been used to parboil root vegetables such as daikon radish, carrots and turnips; it has a subtle sweetness that greatly enhances the flavors of other ingredients. However, purely vegetable-based stocks are lighter in flavor than animal-based ones. You can use fermented foods such as soy sauce or miso paste to boost the umami, and you can add richness with ingredients such as ground sesame seeds. I believe that Zen vegan food centers on using limited ingredients to create delicious and satisfying dishes.

No strong-smelling vegetables are used

There are five types of strong-smelling vegetable that are not allowed in Buddhist temple cuisine, as they are believed to overstimulate the senses: green onions, scallions or leeks; onions; garlic chives; garlic bulbs; and *rakkyo* (*Allium chinense*, a vegetable that is similar to a shallot). The smell of one's breath after eating these vegetables can clash with the fragrance of incense inside a monastery or temple, and may distract from the words of a lecture or sermon. In addition, the stimulation these vegetables are believed to provide may make one more susceptible to worldly desires, and get in the way of a monk's training.

No dairy products are used

In traditional Buddhist cuisine, dairy products such as milk, cheese, cream and butter cannot be used. Even though they are forbidden, sometimes I find myself imagining how delicious a particular dish would be with a little cheese sprinkled on top. Of course, dairy products are used frequently in Italian cuisine, but the Zen vegan Italian dishes in the final chapter of this book do not contain any dairy. I struggled a lot when I was creating those recipes, but it was similar to the struggle everyone faces when trying to create dishes at home with whatever is in the refrigerator. Cooking every day can be hard work, but ideally we want to find joy and comfort in the task, too.

Zen Vegan Food at Fukushoji Temple

At our temple, Fukushoji, near Tokyo, we hold several events throughout the year so that Zen vegan food can be enjoyed by as many people as possible. The following are some important aspects of temple life.

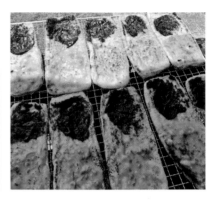

Washing the Bowl
After a meal, a slice of *takuan* pickled daikon radish is placed in the rice bowl, and roasted green tea is added. The tea is drunk, leaving the bowl clean, and the takuan is chewed slowly and quietly.

Seasonal Dishes
Special Zen vegan menus are created to correspond with seasonal events or Buddhist traditions. The summer menu shown here was served during the June rainy season.

Zen Vegan Festival Foods
Sometimes we provide Zen vegan food to other temples for their festivals, like this tofu dish with a savory-sweet sauce called *kitsune dengaku* we made for Shinkomyoji Temple in Shizuoka City, at their Kasamori Inarirei festival.

Buddhist Chanting Before Meals
After an explanation of the eating etiquette taught in the Tendai school of Buddhism, all the participants chant together before the meal. This is a form of prayer in Buddhism.

Cooking Events
I also run the Town Temple School Project at Fukushoji Temple. The project holds Zen vegan cooking events, zazen meditation sessions, Buddhist sculpture workshops and more, to help people become more familiar with Buddhism.

A Glossary of Ingredients

tofu

kombu
seaweed

7 spice blend
Called *shichimi togarashi* in Japanese, this is a ready-made Japanese condiment containing a mixture of seven spices. You can find it in Asian grocery stores.

Abura-age deep-fried tofu
These flat, light-brown rectangles are made of deep-fried tofu. Tofu puffs, used in Chinese cuisine, are similar and may be used instead. Abura-age can be found ready-made in Japanese grocery stores, often in the freezer section. Place in a colander and pour boiling water over to remove excess oil. Drain well before using.

Burdock root
Burdock root, called *gobo* in Japanese, is a long, thin fibrous root vegetable. It's available at Asian grocery stores.

Chinese yam
Several recipes in this book call for yamato yam, which can be hard to find outside Japan. Chinese yam (called *nagaimo* in Japanese) is more easily available in Asian grocery stores around the world. Chinese Yam is a long, light beige root with a more watery texture than yamato yam, so you may need to drain off excess moisture after grating.

Flour
In this book, both high-gluten bread flour and low-gluten cake flour are used for a crispy finish on fried foods. All-purpose flour can be substituted in either case.

Kombu seaweed
This thick, flavorful seaweed is so valued in Japanese culture that in the past it was even used to pay taxes! To this day it is placed on the altar at Shinto shrines as an offering to the gods. Kombu is widely utilized in Zen vegan cooking. Not only is it an ingredient in various dishes, but dashi stock made with kombu is foundational to many recipes.

Konnyaku
Also called devil's-tongue jelly, konnyaku is a gelatinous block of yam made from the corm of the konjac plant. It can be found at Japanese grocery stores. Drain off the water from the package, briefly parboil and drain again to get rid of the odor before using.

Mirin
This sweet liquid flavoring is made by mixing inoculated steamed rice with *shochu* distilled spirits, then fermenting for a month or two. Mirin is a key component of Zen vegan cooking, adding sweetness and a shiny finish. Although it is primarily used as a cooking ingredient, high-quality mirin is also a beverage. It is drunk at New Year's as a festive toast for good health and longevity.

Miso
Miso proved to be a more than satisfying substitute for cheese in the Italian chapter of this book. Even though they come from different food cultures, both cheese and miso are aged, fermented foods with many common features. You can choose any type of miso you like for the recipes in this book.

Mitsuba
This fresh green herb is often used in traditional Japanese cuisine. If you can't find it, substitute mizuna greens or flat-leaf parsley.

Mixed grains *see* **Zakkoku**

Nagaimo *see* **Chinese yam**

Natto
Natto is cooked soybeans that have been fermented with the bacillus that grows on rice straw. It is rather pungent and is an acquired taste, but is highly nutritious and well worth getting to like. Natto is available in ready-to-eat packets at Japanese or Asian grocery stores and some health food stores.

Nori Seaweed
This laver has been stretched out into sheets and dried. The best nori has a green-black color. This is the seaweed that's used for sushi rolls. You can find it in many regular supermarkets as well as at Japanese grocery stores

Red bean paste
This is a sweet paste made from adzuki beans. It can be found in both chunky (*tsubu-an*) and smooth (*koshi-an*) form. Ready-made versions of both are available at well-stocked Japanese grocery stores or online.

Rice-rinsing water

As the name suggests, this is the cloudy water that comes from rinsing uncooked rice grains. Rice is generally rinsed in three or four changes of water before it is cooked. When rice-rinsing water is called for in a recipe, use the water from the second rinse.

Salt

Salt is much revered in Japanese culture, and holds a special status. For example, it is used to purify the ring before every bout at a sumo tournament. Salt is essential for bringing out the subtle flavors of Zen vegan food, and the best available quality should be used.

Sansho pepper

An aromatic spice with a citrus zing, ground sansho pepper is made from the seed pods of the Japanese prickly-ash tree. It is available at Japanese grocery stores or online.

Sesame oil

Both dark sesame oil (made from toasted sesame seeds) and light sesame oil (made from raw seeds) are used in this book. The strong, nutty fragrance of dark sesame oil really stimulates the appetite, and is ideal for stir-fries. Light sesame oil is well suited for dressings and marinades due to its unassertive flavor. Light sesame oil can be found in some health-food stores, and dark sesame oil is available at Asian grocery stores.

Sesame paste

The pronounced nutty flavor of Japanese sesame paste comes from roasted sesame seeds. If you can't find it at your local Japanese grocery store, substitute tahini, Chinese sesame paste or unsweetened peanut butter.

Sesame seeds

According to one legend, sesame seeds came over to Japan from mainland Asia at the same time as Buddhism. That alone makes them seem closely connected to Zen vegan cooking. Nutritionally speaking, these seeds are packed with sesamin, fats and more. Choose either the white (light brown) or black type according to your preference.

Shiitake mushrooms

Both fresh and dried shiitake mushrooms are indispensable to Zen vegan cooking. If you have time, try boosting the flavor of fresh shiitake mushrooms by placing them in the sun with the undersides facing up for a while.

Shio kombu

Shio kombu is seaweed cooked in a salty-sweet mixture of soy sauce and mirin and then dried. It can be found online and in Asian markets.

Shiso leaf

Also called beefsteak plant or perilla, shiso is a fresh-tasting herb that is used extensively in Japanese cooking. It is available at well-stocked Japanese grocery stores—or you can grow your own! Fresh basil leaves or flat-leaf parsley can be substituted.

Soy sauce

Both dark and light soy sauce are used in this book. Dark soy sauce is the rich, dark-brown liquid you may be used to seeing, while light soy sauce is amber colored. Do not confuse light soy sauce with reduced-salt soy sauce! In fact, light soy sauce (*usukuchi shoyu* in Japanese) is actually saltier than dark soy sauce. It is lighter in color because of the additional salt; it is also fermented for a shorter time.

Either kind will work in the recipes in this book.

Umeboshi

These intensely sour salt-pickled fruits are generally referred to as plums, but they are actually a variety of apricot. Find them in Japanese grocery stores or online.

Yamato yam

A starchy root vegetable. When grated it forms a very thick, viscous paste. *See also* **Chinese yam**.

Yuba

Yuba is the delicate skin that is skimmed off the surface of heated soy milk as tofu is being made. Like tofu, it is a valuable source of protein, and can be cooked in several ways. A bestselling tofu cookbook from the Edo period (1603–1868) called *100 Tofu Delicacies* included numerous yuba dishes.

Yuzu citrus

Light orange-yellow yuzu citrus is available in winter at well-stocked Japanese or Korean groceries. Yuzu has a rich, distinctive fragrance. If you can't find it fresh, it is possible to buy bottled yuzu juice in Japanese grocery stores or online. Otherwise, try substituting fresh lemon or lime.

Zakkoku

Ready-mixed grains meant to be cooked with rice, called *zakkoku*, are available at Japanese grocery stores. You can also make your own mix using grains such as millet, barley, quinoa and so on.

Chapter 1
Make-ahead Basics and Snacks

We'll start this chapter with make-ahead basics: Dashi Stock, Seasoned Nori Seaweed and Mushroom Miso Paste. Then we'll show ways to use them in several Zen vegan snack recipes. These staples have ample fragrance and umami, so maximize them by using them as seasoning, part of a dish, a "hidden flavor" supporting the main flavors, and so on.

Two Kinds of Dashi Stock

In order to bring out the subtle flavors in vegetables, dashi stock is essential.

Kombu Dashi Stock

Note that if you need to wipe any dirt or sand off the surface of the kombu beforehand, be sure not to wipe off the white powdery coating with it. This is a substance called mannitol, a sugar alcohol, which contains both umami and sweetness and gives great flavor to your dashi stock.

MAKES ABOUT 4 CUPS (1 L)

Piece of dried kombu seaweed, approximately 6 x 3 inches (15 x 7.5 cm)
4 cups (1 L) water

1 Soak the kombu in the water until pliable.

2 Simmer over low heat for 30 minutes. Raise the heat at the end and take out the kombu just before the liquid comes to a boil. (Reserve this kombu for use in other recipes—you may want to increase the size of the kombu piece depending on how much you need for another recipe.) Alternatively put the kombu and water in a closed container and refrigerate overnight.

Shiitake Mushroom Dashi Stock

Zen vegan dishes tend to be lightly flavored, and the strong umami of dried shiitake mushrooms has a very distinctive note. That strong flavor can overwhelm other ingredients, so be sure to combine it with Kombu Dashi Stock (see this page) or the liquid from cooking vegetables to soften and balance it out.

MAKES ABOUT 4 CUPS (1 L)

5 dried shiitake mushrooms
Cold water for initial rinsing and soaking
4 cups (1 L) water

1 Rinse the shiitake and soak in cold water for about 30 minutes.

2 Discard the initial soaking water, put the shiitake in the 4 cups of water and refrigerate overnight.

3 Remove the shiitake mushrooms from the water and bring the liquid to a boil before using.

Seasoned Nori Seaweed

Tsukudani refers to a type of savory preserved food in Japanese cuisine in which various ingredients are simmered slowly in a mixture of soy sauce and sugar. Nori seaweed simmered in this way is one of the oldest and most popular types of *tsukudani*. It's a staple breakfast item in Japan, eaten with hot steamed rice. Occasionally, I get an uncontrollable urge to eat some seasoned nori.

Nori seaweed has a very long history. Buddhism was introduced to Japan around the Asuka to Nara periods (538–710). Since this new religion prohibited the killing of living beings, nori, a type of laver, became an invaluable food source, and was considered a blessing from the sea. However, edible seaweeds including nori, kombu and wakame were so valuable that they were accepted in lieu of taxes, and they were beyond the reach of ordinary people. Fast-forward to the Edo period (1603–1868) and the time of the first Tokugawa shogun, Tokugawa Ieyasu. Ieyasu loved nori, and ordered it to be farmed in quantity in what is now Tokyo Bay. Nori from Edo (Tokyo) soon became well known around the nation, as regional lords brought it back with them to their domains. Nori does not have a long shelf life, however, and simmering it with soy sauce and sugar is one way to preserve it. This is how seasoned nori become a popular food that is still enjoyed to this day.

MAKES ABOUT ¾ CUP (185 ml)

10 whole sheets nori seaweed, each sheet 8 x 7
   inches (20 x 18 cm)
Water
3 tablespoons dark soy sauce
3 tablespoons sugar

1 Tear the nori into small pieces and place in a saucepan.

2 Add water to cover and leave for 15 minutes.

3 Turn the heat to low and stir in the sugar.

4 Add the soy sauce, stirring so that the mixture does not stick to the pan.

5 Simmer over low heat until the paste is the consistency of jelly.

A traditional way of extending the life of once-precious nori seaweed

1 Tear up the nori seaweed sheets.

2 Add water.

3 Add the sugar.

4 Add the soy sauce.

5 Simmer and reduce.

Crispy Rice Balls with Seasoned Nori Seaweed

Onigiri rice balls are a basic staple of Japanese cuisine. In this recipe, seasoned nori is mixed into the rice. The rice balls are then wrapped in nori and deep-fried. They are crispy, rich and addictive. I hope you give them a try!

A new take on the classic rice ball

SERVES 2

Piece of firm tofu, about 3½ oz (100 g)
¾ cup (150 g) cooked short-grain rice
2 tablespoons Seasoned Nori Seaweed (see page 13)
1 whole sheet nori, 8 x 7 inches (20 x 18 cm)
Oil, for deep-frying
Salt, to taste

1 Drain the tofu well in a colander. Mix tofu, rice, and seasoned nori in a bowl.

2 Wrap a quarter of the tofu-rice mixture in cling film and squeeze firmly to form a ball. Repeat with remaining mixture to form 4 balls.

3 Cut the nori sheet into quarters. Wrap each rice ball in a piece of nori. Heat oil to 360°F (180°C) oil and fry rice balls until browned and crispy. Serve with salt to taste.

ZEN VEGAN NOTE
Drain the tofu thoroughly by wrapping it in several layers of paper towels and placing it in a colander or a flat sieve with a weight such as a plate on top. Leave for at least 30 minutes, and drain off the excess water. The rice balls can be made with rice only, but the tofu gives them an extra crispy finish and a light, fluffy texture, so I highly recommend adding it.

Baked Potatoes with Seasoned Nori Seaweed

The skin of the potato is actually quite rich in nutrition and flavor, and it is delicious when cooked with care. This dish is baked as though it was a gratin, but doesn't contain any cheese or dairy products!

SERVES 2

2 medium potatoes
2 tablespoons Seasoned Nori Seaweed (see page 13)
4 green shiso leaves
1 teaspoon dark sesame oil

1 Put the potatoes in a microwave-safe container, cover with cling film and microwave on the high setting until tender. Peel while still hot, reserving the peel. Mash the potatoes.

2 Add the seasoned nori to the mashed potatoes and mix well. Spread the mixture in an ovenproof baking dish.

3 Top the potato mixture with alternating layers of potato skin and green shiso leaves, and drizzle the sesame oil over all.

4 Bake in a toaster oven or in an oven preheated to 400°F (200°C) until browned on top.

ZEN VEGAN NOTE
The potato skins are used as a topping for this dish, which is baked until browned and crispy. Making use of the entire ingredient without wasting anything is one of the core concepts of Zen vegan cooking.

Bake until browned to bring out the nutty flavor of the potato skins

Natto Soup with Seasoned Nori Seaweed

Because this soup contains natto (fermented soybeans), it's very filling. It's also very quick to prepare, making it a great option for busy days. The nori adds umami, and both the natto and the ginger warm up the body. This soup is also a good pick-me-up when you are a little tired. Look for natto in the freezer section of your Asian market.

This soup is great comfort food

SERVES 2

1 packet natto, about 1½ oz (45 g)
1¾ cups (425 ml) water
2 tablespoons Seasoned Nori Seaweed (see page 13)
1 slice fresh ginger
½ tablespoon light soy sauce
Salt, to taste
Toasted white sesame seeds, to taste

1 Place the natto in a small bowl and stir well. Combine the water, seasoned nori, natto, ginger and soy sauce in a pan over medium heat and bring to a boil.

2 Taste and season with salt. Sprinkle with sesame seeds before serving.

ZEN VEGAN NOTE
One theory as to how natto gets its name is that it used to be fermented in the storage barns, or *naya*, of temples. Fermentation, which is such an integral part of Japanese cuisine, may have spread around the country along with Buddhism. The more you mix natto and bring out its sticky texture, the more flavor it will have.

Chinese Yam and Avocado with Seasoned Nori Seaweed

The gooey texture of Chinese yam and the richness of avocado are brought together with the gentle flavor of the seasoned nori. As long as you have seasoned nori on hand, this side dish is a snap to make. It works well as an accompaniment to plain rice or as an appetizer with drinks.

SERVES 2

3½ oz (100 g) Chinese yam (nagaimo)
½ avocado
2 tablespoons Seasoned Nori Seaweed (see page 13)
A little hot mustard
Salt, to taste

1 Scrub the Chinese yam well, but do not peel. Cut into ¼-inch (5 mm) cubes. Cut the avocado in half, remove the pit, and scoop the flesh out with a spoon.

2 Combine the yam, avocado and seasoned nori in a bowl. Add the mustard and mix well. Adjust the seasoning with salt.

ZEN VEGAN NOTE
Avocados turn brown very quickly, so cut the avocado just before serving this dish. I think that partaking of a dish as soon as it's prepared expresses the ultimate respect to the ingredients.

Nourishing and packed with flavor

Mushroom Miso Paste

In temperate, humid Japan, it is said that there are more than six thousand varieties of mushrooms. The Japanese people have been enjoying these delicious morsels offered by the earth for a very long time. Is there anything better than sipping hot mushroom broth on a cold winter day? Mushrooms are natural source of guanidylic acid, an amino acid that is rich in umami flavor, so combining several types of mushrooms can really make for a delicious result. In addition, commercially grown mushrooms are available year round, for which I am so grateful.

In this staple recipe, mushrooms are finely chopped and mixed with kombu seaweed, steamed in sake and combined with miso to make a delicious Mushroom Miso Paste that can be used in soups and sauces and many other dishes—have fun experimenting!

A flavorful combination of umami-rich ingredients

MAKES ABOUT 2 CUPS

7 oz (200 g) beech (shimeji) mushrooms
7 oz (200 g) enoki mushrooms
7 oz (200 g) shiitake mushrooms
7 oz (200 g) hen of the woods (maitake) mushrooms
Piece of dried kombu seaweed, 3½ inch (7 cm) square
½ tablespoon salt
3 tablespoons sake
2 tablespoons sugar
2 tablespoons dark sesame oil
½ cup (125 g) miso paste

1 Assemble the mushrooms you will be using. You can put together your own mix.

2 Discard the hard stem ends and chop the mushrooms finely.

3 Combine the chopped mushrooms and kombu seaweed in a large pan over medium heat. Add the salt and sake and let come to a boil. Cover, reduce heat to low and simmer gently for about 10 minutes.

4 Add the sugar to the pan. Adding sugar raises the temperature in the pan, so stir continuously to prevent burning.

5 Add the sesame oil and miso and mix well to incorporate while continuing to cook the mushrooms.

6 Simmer over low heat for about 3 minutes until most of the moisture in the pan has evaporated. Remove the kombu seaweed.

1 Assemble the mushrooms.

2 Chop the mushrooms.

3 Simmer the mushrooms.

4 Add the sugar.

5 Add the sesame oil and miso

6 Cook off the moisture.

Deep-fried Tofu with Mushroom Miso

This is a Zen vegan version of another Japanese classic, called *agedashi dofu* in Japanese. To make the sauce, just thin out the Mushroom Miso Paste with a little kombu dashi stock. Although this tofu dish is usually served with soy sauce, sesame oil–scented miso sauce goes really well with it too.

A delicious sauce is made in no time thanks to Mushroom Miso Paste

SERVES 2

Piece of firm tofu, about 7 oz (200 g)
Cornstarch or potato starch, for coating
Oil, for deep-frying
1 head baby bok choy
4 tablespoons Mushroom Miso Paste (p.18)
¾ cup (185 ml) Kombu Dashi Stock
 (see page 12)
1 teaspoon cornstarch or potato starch,
 dissolved in 2 teaspoons water

1 Drain the tofu well in a colander or on a flat sieve for several minutes. Cut into easy-to-eat pieces. Coat with cornstarch on all sides. Heat the oil to 340°F (170°C) and deep-fry the tofu until lightly browned.

2 Parboil the bok choy. Drain and cool under running water. Squeeze to remove as much liquid as possible.

3 Combine the Mushroom Miso Paste and kombu dashi stock in a pan over medium heat and bring to a boil. Stir in the cornstarch-and-water mixture and continue to cook, stirring, until sauce thickens.

4 Cut the bok choy in half. Arrange the fried tofu and bok choy on a serving plate and spoon the sauce over.

ZEN VEGAN NOTE
The contrast between the crispy coating and the creamy inside is delicious. Contrast and variety in our food is as important as contrast and variety in other aspects of our daily lives!

Apple, Mitsuba and Mushroom Salad

Crisp leafy greens are mixed with an ample dollop of Mushroom Miso Paste in this salad. The dressing will wilt the greens, making them easy to eat and extremely moreish, but don't worry—this dish is quite low in calories!

SERVES 2

2 tablespoons Mushroom Miso Paste (see page 18)
2 tablespoons apple cider vinegar
3 tablespoons light sesame oil
Salt, to taste
2 cups (70 g) leafy greens of your choice
   (I've used green leaf lettuce)
½ medium apple
3½ oz (100 g) mitsuba sprigs or flat-leaf parsley
Toasted white sesame seeds, to taste

1 In a large bowl, combine the Mushroom Miso Paste, vinegar, oil and salt. Mix well to make the dressing.

2 Tear the leafy greens into bite-sized pieces. Slice the apple thinly. Roughly chop the mitsuba.

3 Add the greens, apple and mitsuba to the dressing and toss to mix. Sprinkle with sesame seeds before serving.

ZEN VEGAN NOTE
Apple and mitsuba is a surprisingly delicious combination. Flat-leaf parsley also works well. Appearances can be deceiving, whether it's food or people.

Mushroom Miso Paste adds heft and savor to this salad

Zen Vegan Mapo Tofu

Mapo tofu is a classic spicy tofu dish from Sichuan Province in China that is very popular in Japan. This Zen vegan version has no meat or green onions in it, but the Mushroom Miso Paste and sesame oil give it a satisfying mapo-tofu flavor. This version will delight people who aren't fond of the rich, meaty character of the original dish.

Tofu plus Mushroom Miso Paste equals a great Vegan Mapo Tofu

SERVES 2

Piece of firm tofu, about 7 oz (200 g)
Small piece fresh ginger, about 1 inch (2.5 cm)
2 small red chili peppers
2 tablespoons dark sesame oil
4 tablespoons Mushroom Miso Paste (see page 18)
Scant ½ cup (100 ml) water
2 teaspoons cornstarch or potato starch, dissolved in 4 teaspoons water
Japanese 7 spice blend (shichimi togarashi), to taste

1 Cut the tofu into ½ inch (1.5 cm) cubes. Bring a pan of water to a boil, and cook the tofu cubes in it for 1 minute. Drain well.

2 Chop the ginger finely. Halve the chili peppers lengthwise and remove the calyxes and seeds.

3 Heat the sesame oil in a skillet. Add the ginger and chili peppers and sauté until fragrant. Add the tofu, Mushroom Miso Paste and water, and simmer for 2 minutes over medium heat, stirring continuously.

4 Add the cornstarch-and-water mixture and bring to a boil. Simmer, stirring frequently, until the sauce thickens. Add 7 spice blend to taste.

ZEN VEGAN NOTE
I created this Zen vegan version of mapo tofu because I really craved it during my strict period of training to be a monk, at Mount Hiei. It goes really well with plain rice.

Mushroom Miso Potato Croquettes

These are simple croquettes made with whole potatoes mixed with Mushroom Miso Paste. They are dusted with cornstarch or potato starch instead of breadcrumbs before deep-frying. This not only makes them lower in calories than typical croquettes, but also really brings out the taste of the potatoes.

SERVES 2

2 medium potatoes
½ cup (125 g) Mushroom Miso Paste (see page 18)
Cornstarch or potato starch, for binding and dusting
Oil, for deep-frying

1 Scrub the potatoes but do not peel them. Place in a microwave-safe container. Cover with cling film and microwave on the high setting for about 5 minutes until cooked through.

2 Mash the potatoes with the skin on. Stir in the Mushroom Miso Paste and enough cornstarch to hold the mixture together.

3 Divide the potato mixture into six equal portions and form into oval patties. Dust with cornstarch or potato starch. Heat oil to 360°F (180°C). Fry the croquettes until browned on the outside.

ZEN VEGAN NOTE
If you leave the skin on the potatoes, little bits of it will become crispy when the croquettes are deep-fried, adding texture to the dish.

The combination of potato and Mushroom Miso is simple, yet delicious

Mushroom Miso Paste is versatile because it's not too sweet

Two Types of Miso-glazed Delights

When a grilled or boiled food—often on a skewer—is glazed with a miso sauce, it is called *dengaku* in Japanese. This sauce is often quite sweet, but here I have used Mushroom Miso Paste, which is less sweet and full of umami. These miso-glazed dishes go very well with plain rice.

Miso-glazed Shiitake Mushrooms

SERVES 2

Piece of Chinese yam or yamato yam, about 3 oz (90 g)
4 tablespoons Mushroom Miso Paste (see page 18)
6 large fresh shiitake mushrooms
1 tablespoon dark sesame oil
Toasted black and white sesame seeds

1 Grate the yam, peel and all, into a fine mesh sieve and let drain for a few minutes. Transfer to a bowl. Add the Mushroom Miso and mix well.

2 Cut off the mushroom stems, discarding the tough ends. Place the caps upside down and spoon the yam and miso mixture on top.

3 Arrange the mushroom stems and the filled mushroom caps in a skillet. Add a little water, cover the pan, and cook the mushrooms over low heat until the caps are puffy and tender.

4 Drizzle the sesame oil over the mushrooms and increase heat to medium. Cook until lightly browned. Transfer to a serving plate and sprinkle with the sesame seeds.

✿ ZEN VEGAN NOTE
The word *dengaku* originally referred to a traditional dance to pray for a good rice harvest. By the Edo period (1603–1868) it came to mean the dish with miso sauce that we know today.

Miso-glazed Deep-fried Tofu

SERVES 2

½ ear fresh corn, or 3 oz (90 g) canned corn
2 tablespoons Mushroom Miso Paste (page 18)
1 teaspoon dark soy sauce
2 pieces abura-age deep-fried tofu
4 green shiso leaves, shredded

1 Boil the corn for about 5 minutes. Drain and scrape the kernels off the cob. Combine the kernels with the Mushroom Miso Paste and soy sauce.

2 Spread the corn and miso mixture over the abura-age.

3 Bake in a toaster oven, or in an oven preheated to 400°F (200°C), until slightly charred on top. Serve topped with shredded green shiso leaves.

✿ ZEN VEGAN NOTE
Abura-age is a traditional offering to Inari Okami, a Shinto deity revered in Japan since olden times. Corn is added to this recipe because there are cultural associations between corn and foxes, which are under this deity's special protection.

Chapter 2

Delicious Congee Rice Porridge

An old Buddhist sutra states that congee (called *kayu* in Japanese) has ten merits. It clears up your complexion; it fills you with strength; it extends your lifespan; it's easy to eat; it relieves heartburn; it refreshes your mouth; it prevents you from catching colds; it fills your stomach; it moistens your throat; and it is easy to digest. What other food can claim such benefits? This chapter begins by showing you how to make basic plain congee, followed by some great variations.

Basic Congee Rice Porridge

In Japan, congee is often served at breakfast, but you can eat it any time of the day! Served plain with a dash of salt or soy sauce, it can settle an upset stomach. For a simple, delicious congee, add toasted sesame seeds, a drizzle of sesame oil, or crumbled nori seaweed. Dressed up or down, it's a standby that you'll return to again and again.

SERVES 2

¾ cup (150 g) uncooked short-grain rice
Water for rinsing and soaking
2¾ cups (700 ml) water, for cooking
Salt, to taste

1 Rinse the rice in several changes of water. Soak in enough water to cover for 15 minutes. Transfer to a colander and let drain for 15 minutes.

2 Bring the water to a boil in a medium saucepan over high heat. When it boils, add the drained rice and the salt.

3 Return the liquid to a boil. Stir up the rice from the bottom of the pan once, then reduce heat to low, so that the surface of the water is just bubbling gently. Simmer for 10 minutes. If you stir the rice too much, the surface of the grains will become damaged and the final results will not look very appetizing, so be careful.

4 Cover the pan with a lid, turn off the heat and leave the rice to continue cooking with residual heat. The rice grains will be separate yet plump and shiny.

1 Rinse the rice, and put it into boiling water.

2 Simmer, so that the water is bubbling gently.

3 Cover and allow to keep cooking in residual heat.

A perfect pick-me-up

A luxurious congee with fragrant roasted sesame seeds

Congee with Pickled Plum and Egyptian Spinach

This congee is a great restorative when you're feeling tired. The salty tang of umeboshi pickled plums is perfectly complemented by the Egyptian spinach (also called molokhia). You can also use regular spinach or chard.

SERVES 2

½ cup (100 g) fresh Egyptian spinach
1 tablespoon dark soy sauce
2 servings Basic Congee (see page 26)
2 umeboshi salt-pickled plum, pitted and chopped.

1 Bring a pot of water to a boil. Blanch the Egyptian spinach for 2 to 3 minutes. Drain and cool under cold running water. Squeeze to remove moisture, cut into bite-sized pieces, and mix with the soy sauce.

2 Ladle the congee into two bowls. Arrange the Egyptian spinach on top and finish with a dollop of chopped umeboshi.

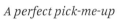

ZEN VEGAN NOTE
The refreshing sourness of umeboshi and the highly nutritious Egyptian spinach with its unique slippery texture combine to make this a very comforting dish.

Sesame Salt Congee

Toasting sesame seeds just before they are served makes them really nutty and fragrant. Sesame seeds are a highly prized ingredient in Zen vegan cooking. Just a small amount can transform a dish.

SERVES 2

3 tablespoons raw white sesame seeds
2 scant tablespoons (30 g) salt
2 servings Basic Congee (see page 26)

1 Put the sesame seeds in a dry skillet over low heat. Toast them slowly, stirring frequently, until they emit a nutty fragrance. Mix with the salt. If desired, crush seeds and salt together with a mortar and pestle to release more flavor.

2 Ladle the congee into two bowls. Top each serving with a spoonful of the sesame salt mixture from Step 1.

ZEN VEGAN NOTE
Crushing freshly toasted sesame seeds makes them even more fragrant and delicious. Take a moment to calm your spirit with their scent before quietly savoring this meal.

"Eel" Congee with Kabayaki Sauce

In Japan, freshwater eel is typically eaten in dish called *kabayaki*, where eel is grilled over charcoal and served with a savory-sweet sauce. In this Zen vegan version, the "eel" is made from deep-fried tofu. The flavorful sauce and the fragrant nori melt into the congee, making each bite more delicious than the last.

A traditional Buddhist "imitation" dish

ZEN VEGAN NOTE
We serve this dish every year at our temple on the midsummer Day of the Ox, a holiday on which eel kabayaki is traditionally served. Eat this slowly, savoring every bite, and you may begin to think this is actually eel, not a Zen vegan version. Such moments make my efforts feel worthwhile.

SERVES 2

Piece of firm tofu, about 4 oz (120 g)
Piece of Chinese yam or yamato yam, about 4 oz (120 g)
Piece of burdock root, about 2 oz (50 g)
2 tablespoons cornstarch or potato starch
Salt, to taste

For the kabayaki sauce
2 tablespoons dark soy sauce
2 tablespoons sugar
6½ tablespoons mirin

1 whole sheet nori seaweed, 8 x 7 inches (20 x 18 cm)
Oil for deep-frying
2 servings Basic Congee (see page 26)
Japanese 7 spice blend (shichimi togarashi), to taste

1 Drain the tofu well by wrapping it in several layers of paper towels and placing it in a colander or on a flat sieve with a weight (such as a plate) on top for about 30 minutes. Scrub the yam and burdock root but do not peel. Grate into a bowl.

2 Crumble the tofu. Add the tofu, cornstarch and salt to the grated roots and mix well.

3 Combine the kabayaki sauce ingredients in a small pan and bring to a boil over medium heat, stirring frequently.

4 Cut the nori into six equal pieces. Spread a sixth of the tofu and vegetable mixture evenly across a piece of nori. Repeat with the remaining nori pieces. Heat the oil to 340°F (170°C). Fry the pieces, placing them in the oil nori side first, until lightly browned. Drain well and cover with the sauce.

5 Ladle the congee into two bowls and top each one with pieces of deep-fried "eel." Sprinkle with 7 spice blend before serving.

Whole Corn Congee

Sweet corn is popular with all ages, but few people know how much flavor the cob holds. Congee that has absorbed the delicious umami of the cob is topped with kernels that have been stir-fried in toasty soy sauce.

SERVES 2

¾ cup (150 g) uncooked short-grain rice
Water for washing and soaking
½ ear sweet corn
2¾ cups (700 ml) water, for cooking
2 green shiso leaves
Sesame oil
½ tablespoon dark soy sauce

1 Rinse the rice in several changes of water. Soak in enough water to cover for 15 minutes. Transfer to a fine-mesh sieve and allow to drain.

2 Scrape the kernels off the corn cob with a knife. Setting the kernels aside, bring the 2¾ cups of water and the corn cob to a boil in a saucepan over high heat. Add the rice and cook according to the directions for Basic Congee on page 26.

3 Cut the shiso leaves into thin shreds. Heat the sesame oil in a skillet, add the reserved corn kernels and stir-fry over high heat. Add the soy sauce and stir rapidly. Set aside.

4 Ladle the congee into two bowls. Add corn kernels to each bowl and top with the shredded shiso leaves.

ZEN VEGAN NOTE
Fresh corn cobs make a delicious stock. One of the basic tenets of Zen vegan cooking is to demonstrate gratitude for our food by not wasting any part of it. This congee is perfectly suited to that way of thinking.

The sweetness of the corn permeates the rice

Soy Milk Congee with Konnyaku

This mild, creamy dish is a vegan version of a famous congee called Siddhartha's Milk Congee. Legend has it that the Lord Siddhartha was eating the congee when he achieved enlightenment.

This congee may not bring enlightenment, but it's guaranteed to bring enjoyment

SERVES 2

¾ cup (150 g) uncooked short-grain rice
Water for rinsing and soaking
1 scant cup (225 ml) unsweetened soy milk
1¾ cups (425 ml) Kombu Dashi Stock (see page 12)
Pinch of salt
Piece of konnyaku, about 3½ oz (100 g)
1 small red chili pepper
1 tablespoon dark sesame oil
1 tablespoon light soy sauce
1 tablespoon mirin

1 Rinse the rice several times. Cover with water and soak for 15 minutes. Transfer to a fine-mesh sieve and allow to drain.

2 Bring the soy milk and dashi stock to a boil in a saucepan over high heat. Add the rice and salt. Cook according to the directions for Basic Congee on page 26.

3 Blanch the konnyaku in boiling water for 60 seconds. Drain and cool. Tear the konnyaku into bite-sized pieces with a spoon. Discard the calyx and seeds from the chili pepper and chop finely.

4 Heat the sesame oil in a skillet. Add the konnyaku and chili pepper and sauté over medium heat. Add the soy sauce and mirin and remove from heat.

5 Ladle the congee into two bowls. Serve topped with konnyaku and chili pepper.

ZEN VEGAN NOTE
Konnyaku, a gelatinous block made from the corm of the konjac plant, is high in water-soluble fiber, making it good for digestion and for removing any bitterness from food it's cooked with. Some regions of Japan have a custom of offering konnyaku to Enma, god of the underworld, to cleanse the person making the offering of evil thoughts.

Seared Carrot Congee

Peeled carrot is grated and cooked with the congee rice, while the peel is browned in light sesame oil and used as a topping. This is another example of how different parts of a single vegetable can be cooked in different ways to create very different flavors.

SERVES 2

¾ cup (150 g) uncooked short-grain rice
Water for rinsing and soaking
1 medium carrot
2¾ cups (700 ml) Kombu Dashi Stock (see page 12)
Pinch of salt
½ tablespoon light sesame oil

1 Rinse the rice in several changes of water. Soak in enough water to cover for 15 minutes. Transfer to a fine-mesh sieve and allow to drain.

2 Peel the carrot, reserving the peel. Grate the peeled carrot.

3 Bring the kombu dashi stock and the grated carrot to a boil in a saucepan over high heat. Add the rice and salt. Cook according to the directions for Basic Congee on page 26

4 Heat the sesame oil in a skillet. Pan-fry the carrot peel over medium heat until browned.

5 Ladle the congee into two bowls and top with the carrot peel.

ZEN VEGAN NOTE
Fry the carrot peel until it's browned and crisp so that no part of the carrot is wasted. You can also try using olive oil instead of sesame oil.

The beautiful color of this congee warms the spirit

Yuba Congee

Yuba is the soft skin that forms on top of heated soy milk when tofu is made. It melts as it is cooked with the rice, imparting a rich texture to the congee. The assertive topping is arugula mixed with natto (fermented soybeans).

Yuba gives this congee a rich and creamy texture

SERVES 2

¾ cup (150 g) uncooked short-grain rice
Water for rinsing and soaking
2¾ cups (700 ml) Kombu Dashi Stock (see page 12)
3 oz (90 g) fresh yuba
Salt, to taste
1 packet natto, about 1½ oz (45 g)
3 cups (60 g) roughly chopped arugula
½ tablespoon light soy sauce

1 Rinse the rice in several changes of water. Soak in enough water to cover for 15 minutes. Transfer to a fine-mesh sieve and allow to drain.

2 Bring the kombu dashi stock to a boil in a saucepan over high heat. Add the yuba, rice and salt. Cook according to the directions for Basic Congee on page 26.

3 Mix the natto well so it becomes sticky. Add the arugula and mix to combine. Stir in the soy sauce.

4 Divide the congee between two serving bowls. Top with the arugula-natto mix.

ZEN VEGAN NOTE
There is an old children's song about the monks who live on Mount Hiei near Kyoto. In the song, a child asks a monk what he is eating; the monk replies that he is having grilled yuba dipped in soy sauce along with pickled daikon radish.

Adzuki Bean Congee with Shio Kombu

The first written mention of this very traditional congee appears in the *Tosa Nikki*, a diary written by the poet Ki no Tsurayuki in 935. He writes that he "ate adzuki bean congee for breakfast on Sho-shogatsu [Little New Year, or January 15 on the old calendar]." This congee has been well loved in Japan for a very long time.

SERVES 2

2 tablespoons dried adzuki beans
¾ cup (150 g) uncooked short-grain rice
Water for rinsing and soaking
2¾ cups (700 ml) Kombu Dashi Stock (see page 12)
Salt, to taste
Shio kombu seaweed, for garnish

1 Soak the adzuki beans in water overnight. Rinse and drain well.

2 Rinse the rice in several changes of water. Soak in enough water to cover for 15 minutes. Transfer to a fine-mesh sieve and allow to drain.

3 Combine the kombu dashi stock and adzuki beans in a saucepan and bring to a boil over high heat. Add the rice and the salt. Cook according to the directions for Basic Congee on page 26.

4 Ladle the congee into two bowls and top with the shio kombu.

ZEN VEGAN NOTE
On the old Japanese lunar calendar, the 15th day of the first month was marked by the first full moon of the year. A a full moon was considered very auspicious, that day came to be called Little New Year, and adzuki-bean congee was eaten to drive away evil spirits.

A very comforting traditional congee

Stir-fried Cabbage and Mixed Grain Congee

The browned, stir-fried cabbage brings out the sweetness of the rice. The added texture of the mixed grains is quite addictive. This is a healthy yet hearty congee.

The sweetness of the cabbage balances the mixed grains perfectly

SERVES 2

¾ cup (150 g) uncooked short-grain rice
Water for rinsing and soaking
¼ head green cabbage, about 8 oz (220 g)
1 tablespoon sesame oil
Salt, to taste
3 cups (750 ml) water, for cooking
2 tablespoons mixed grains (zakkoku)

1 Rinse the rice in several changes of water. Soak in enough water to cover for 15 minutes. Transfer to a fine-mesh sieve and allow to drain.

2 Cut the cabbage into bite-sized pieces. Heat the sesame oil in a skillet, add the cabbage and sprinkle with salt. Sauté over medium heat until the cabbage is wilted.

3 Put the 3 cups water in a pan and bring to a boil over high heat. Add the rice, mixed grains and cabbage and cook according to the directions for Basic Congee on page 26.

4 Ladle the congee into two bowls to serve.

ZEN VEGAN NOTE
Mixed grains add nutrition, texture and color to plain rice. It's rather similar to human relationships: when people from different background mix together, the group becomes much better.

Anything Goes Congee

This congee takes its inspiration from a traditional Japanese dish called *yosenabe*, in which various ingredients are cooked together in a hot pot. I've used turnips, carrots, shiitake mushrooms and konnyaku here, but you can use whatever you have on hand or feel like using.

SERVES 2

¾ cup (150 g) uncooked short-grain rice
Water for rinsing and soaking
1 small Asian or baby turnip, with greens
¼ medium carrot
1 shiitake mushroom
Piece of konnyaku, about 2 oz (60 g)
2¾ cups (700 ml) Kombu Dashi Stock (see page 12)
Salt, to taste
Toasted sesame seeds, to taste

1 Rinse the rice in several changes of water. Soak in enough water to cover for 15 minutes. Transfer to a fine-mesh sieve and allow to drain.

2 Remove the turnip greens, reserving any that are edible. Quarter the turnip without peeling, and slice thinly. Quarter the carrot and slice thinly. Remove the tough stem end from the shiitake and cut the cap and stem into quarters. Cut the konnyaku into thin slices ½ inch (1.5 cm) square.

3 Bring the kombu dashi to a boil in a saucepan over high heat. Add the rice, salt, carrots, turnip, konnyaku, shiitake and any other harder vegetables. Cook according to the directions for Basic Congee on page 26. Add greens and tender vegetables just before turning off the heat at the end.

4 Ladle the congee into two bowls and serve sprinkled with sesame seeds.

This congee tastes different every time you make it

ZEN VEGAN NOTE
Use any vegetables you have around; just chop them up and simmer them gently. The character of this congee changes depending on what you might have in your refrigerator.

New Potato and Burdock Root Congee

The tender skins of freshly harvested new potatoes peel off effortlessly as they are washed, leaving a fresh smell. Burdock root also has a wonderfully earthy flavor. The two root vegetables are stir-fried before being added to the congee.

This congee is filled with satisfying, earthy flavors

SERVES 2

¾ cup (150 g) uncooked short-grain rice
Water for rinsing and soaking
1 new potato
Piece of burdock root, about 2 inches (5 cm)
    long
A few springs of mitsuba or parsley
1 tablespoon dark sesame oil
Salt, to taste
2¾ cups (700 ml) water, for cooking
½ tablespoon miso paste
Toasted sesame seeds, to taste

1 Rinse the rice in several changes of water. Soak in enough water to cover for 15 minutes. Transfer to a fine-mesh sieve and allow to drain.

2 Scrub the potato and the burdock root, but do not peel. Cut the potato and burdock root into small pieces. Chop the mitsuba coarsely.

3 Heat the sesame oil in a skillet. Add the potato and burdock root, sprinkle with the salt and sauté over medium heat until they soften slightly.

4 Bring the water and the stir-fried potato and burdock to a boil over high heat in a saucepan. Add the drained rice and cook according to the directions for Basic Congee on page 26. Stir in the miso just before the congee is done.

5 Ladle the congee into two bowls. Top with the mitsuba and sesame seeds.

Mixed Mushroom Congee

The rich variety of mushroom flavors in this congee give it a deep, complex and delicious taste. Because the mushroom flavors are so dominant, the seasoning is kept simple.

SERVES 2

¾ cup (150 g) uncooked short-grain rice
Water for rinsing and soaking
1 oz (30 g) beech (shimeji) mushrooms
1 oz (30 g) enoki mushrooms
1 oz (30 g) hen of the woods (maitake) mushrooms
2 shiitake mushrooms
2¾ cups (700 ml) Kombu Dashi Stock (see page 12)
1 tablespoon light soy sauce
1 tablespoon mirin
Salt, to taste
A few thin slices of citrus zest (sudachi, yuzu, lime or lemon)

1 Rinse the rice in several changes of water. Soak in enough water to cover for 15 minutes. Transfer to a fine-mesh sieve and allow to drain.

2 Discard the stem ends from the mushrooms. Cut the stems into thin rounds and the caps into bite-sized pieces.

3 Combine the kombu dashi stock, mushrooms, soy sauce and mirin in a saucepan and bring to a boil over medium-high heat. Add the rice and cook according to the directions for Basic Congee on page 26. Season with salt, to taste.

4 Ladle the congee into two bowls. Top with thin slices of citrus zest.

ZEN VEGAN NOTE
Mushrooms, the blessing of autumn, should be cooked in one of two ways: very quickly over high heat, or very gently for a long time over low heat to draw out the flavors. Cook this delicious mushroom congee with a calm heart.

This is a great congee to make in fall, when mushrooms are abundant

Congee with Chinese Yam

Finely grated Chinese yam is great with freshly made congee. Take a spoonful with just the Chinese yam first, then with the nori, then the wasabi, to savor each change of flavor.

An energy-boosting congee

SERVES 2

Piece of Chinese yam or yamato yam, unpeeled, about 4 oz (120 g)
2 tablespoons Kombu Dashi Stock (see page 12)
1 tablespoon light soy sauce
2 servings Basic Congee (see page 26)
Freshly grated wasabi or ready-made wasabi paste, to taste
½ nori sheet 4 x 3½ inches (10 x 9 cm), torn into bite-sized pieces

1 Grate the yam, skin and all. Mix with the dashi stock and soy sauce.

2 Ladle the congee into two bowls. Pour the grated yam mixture over, then top with the wasabi and shredded nori.

ZEN VEGAN NOTE
If you can find yamato yam, try using it for this recipe. This nutrient-rich yam used to be called "eel of the mountain" because, like eel, it was believed to give you energy and even make you younger! For fans of its thick, gooey texture, yamato yam is addictive, and goes well with piping hot congee.

Ginger Congee with Deep-fried Tofu

The finely shredded ginger in this congee warms you up from the inside out as you eat. The ready-made abura-age deep-fried tofu for the topping can be found in your Japanese grocery store.

SERVES 2

Small piece fresh ginger, 1 inch (2.5 cm) long
¾ cup (150 g) uncooked short-grain rice
Water for rinsing and soaking
2¾ cups (700 ml) water, for cooking
Salt, to taste
1 piece abura-age deep-fried tofu
Bunch komatsuna greens (or Swiss chard, baby bok choy or spinach), about 5 oz (150 g)
Soy sauce, to taste

1 Cut the ginger into thin slivers. Cook Basic Congee according to the directions on page 26, adding the ginger to the rice cooking water.

2 Pan-fry the piece of abura-age in a dry skillet (no oil added) until browned and crispy on both sides. Cut in half.

3 Parboil the greens in salted water. Drain, cool and cut up roughly.

4 Stir the cooked greens into the congee. Ladle into two bowls. Top each serving with the half piece of abura-age drizzled with a little soy sauce.

The ginger in this congee warms body and soul

ZEN VEGAN NOTE
According to Chinese legend, the Yan Emperor, who is regarded as the father of traditional medicine, once accidentally ate some poisonous mushrooms. As he keeled over, he grabbed a ginger plant growing nearby and ate it and was cured. This is why the character used to write "ginger" in both Chinese and Japanese combines the characters for "life" and the family name of the emperor.

Seasonal Rice Porridges

Zen Vegan Cooking and the Seasons

In Japan, with its distinct seasons, taking seasonality into account is a natural part of everyday life. But sometimes it's hard to keep up with the rapid changes: New Year's is over before you know it, the cherry blossoms scatter, and then the seas are filled with jellyfish, and suddenly winter illuminations are shining . . . how quickly a year flies by!

These days, you can obtain most ingredients at any time of year, but ones that are in season (*shun* 旬 in Japanese) are especially delicious and full of nutrition. If you deconstruct the kanji character for *shun* you can read it as "ten days." This is connected to the idea that the peak seasonality of any ingredient lasts for just ten days.

Even though modern life keeps us all very busy, let's try to appreciate those peak ten days, and to treasure ingredients that are in season.

*Roasted soybeans make a tasty
base for this congee*

*Serve this chilled to get through
a hot summer's day*

Spring Soybean and Millet Congee

The Japanese festival called Setsubun, in February, is the day before the start of spring. It is celebrated by throwing roasted soybeans at people wearing devil masks to drive away harmful spirits. In this congee, roasted soybeans are cooked with the rice, infusing the porridge with a nutty umami. Millet, offering vitamin B$_1$ and polyphenol, makes this dish even healthier.

SERVES 2

¾ cup (150 g) uncooked short-grain rice
Water for rinsing and soaking
¼ cup (50 g) dried soybeans
3¼ cups (800 ml) water
1½ tablespoons dry millet
Salt, to taste

1 Rinse the rice in several changes of water. Cover with water and soak for 15 minutes. Transfer to a fine-mesh sieve and allow to drain for 15 minutes.

2 Roast the soybeans in a dry skillet over medium heat, rolling them around until the skins pop. (If you are using pre-roasted soybeans that are available at Setsubun in Japan, you don't need to do this.)

3 Bring the 3¼ cups of water and the roasted soybeans to a boil in a saucepan over high heat. When the water comes to a boil, add the rinsed rice, millet and salt. Cook according to the recipe for Basic Congee on page 26.

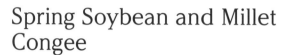

ZEN VEGAN NOTE
The Japanese traditionally believed that gods resided in soybeans. Soybeans are therefore scattered at Setsubun to drive away bad spirits, admonish ourselves and attract good fortune. I've added millet to this congee as a nod to the Japanese folktale *Momotaro* (Peach Boy). where the hero uses millet dumplings to persuade others to help him defeat a band of ogres.

Summer Tomato and Roasted Tea Congee

Hojicha, or slow-roasted green tea, has a wonderful toasty flavor and a slight bitterness that goes very well with the umami of tomato. I've simplified this recipe by using tomato juice, which has a concentrated tomato flavor.

SERVES 2

¾ cup (150 g) uncooked short-grain rice
Water for rinsing and soaking
¾ cup (185 ml) salt-free tomato juice
1 hojicha teabag
2 cups (500 ml) Kombu Dashi Stock (see page 12)
½ tablespoon light soy sauce
Salt, to taste

1 Rinse the rice in several changes of water. Cover with water and soak for 15 minutes. Transfer to a fine-mesh sieve and allow to drain for 15 minutes.

2 Combine the tomato juice, hojicha teabag and dashi stock in a saucepan and bring to a boil over high heat. Remove the teabag.

3 Add the rice, soy sauce and salt to the pan. Cook according to the recipe for Basic Congee on page 26. Serve hot or chilled.

ZEN VEGAN NOTE
Hojicha was invented in the 1920s by roasting tea leaves, stems and twigs in a porcelain pot over charcoal. This method, with its wonderful fragrance, remains the same today. Try this congee well chilled on a hot summer's day.

Eggplants are believed to drive away evil spirits

Improve your luck by eating vegetables ending with "n"

Fall Eggplant and Ginger Congee

In Japan, *zakkoku* mixed grains are often added to rice for extra nutrition and flavor. These grains often include millet, amaranth, quinoa and pressed barley. This congee also contains deep-fried eggplant. The fragrance of the ginger really whets the appetite.

SERVES 2

¾ cup (150 g) uncooked short-grain rice
Water for rinsing and soaking
2 small Japanese or Asian eggplants
Oil for deep-frying
2¾ cups (700 ml) water
2 tablespoons mixed grains (zakkoku)
2 tablespoons finely shredded fresh ginger
½ tablespoon dark soy sauce

ZEN VEGAN NOTE
In the old Japanese calendar, the ninth day of the ninth month is called the Double Ninth Festival. It was believed that eating eggplants on days with a 9 in them helped to prevent strokes.

1 Rinse the rice in several changes of water. Soak in enough water to cover for 15 minutes. Transfer to a fine-mesh sieve and allow to drain for 15 minutes.

2 Slice the eggplants into rounds and dry well with paper towels.

3 Heat the oil to 340°F (170°C). Deep-fry the eggplant rounds until tender.

4 Bring the 2¾ cups of water to a boil in a medium saucepan over high heat. Add the rice, mixed grains, fried eggplant, ginger and soy sauce, and cook according to the directions for Basic Congee on page 26.

5 Serve the congee in bowls.

Winter Solstice Good-luck Congee

It is said that eating foods ending in "n" at the winter solstice brings good fortune. Here I have included kabocha squash (also called *nankin* in Japanese), daikon radish and carrot (*ninjin*). Envision happiness in the coming year as you enjoy this congee.

SERVES 2

¾ cup (150 g) uncooked short-grain rice
Water for rinsing and soaking
5 oz (150 g) kabocha squash
2 oz (50 g) daikon radish
2 oz (50 g) carrot
2¾ cups (700 ml) Kombu Dashi Stock (see page 12)
Pinch of salt
1 tablespoon miso paste
Yuzu juice, to taste

ZEN VEGAN NOTE
It is believed that the sun's energy starts to rise again after the winter solstice, so this day is considered to be a time of good fortune. Even if it's been a bad year, we have a chance to rewind and restart, for which we can be grateful.

1 Rinse the rice in several changes of water. Soak in enough water to cover for 15 minutes. Transfer to a fine-mesh sieve and allow to drain for 15 minutes.

2 Remove the pith and seeds from the kabocha squash. Peel, reserving the peel, and cut the flesh into cubes. Steam until tender and mash coarsely.

3 Quarter the daikon and carrot lengthwise, then slice crosswise. Cut the kabocha peel into bite-sized pieces.

4 Combine the kombu dashi stock, mashed kabocha squash, daikon, carrot and salt in a pan over high heat and bring to a boil. Add the rice and cook according to the directions for Basic Congee on page 26.

5 Stir in the miso when the congee is done. Taste and adjust the seasoning. Serve in bowls, adding yuzu juice as desired.

Seven Herb Congee

This traditional Japanese dish is given a modern twist with Western greens. This congee is topped with mochi, pounded glutinous rice, formed into cakes. It's sold in dried form at Japanese or Asian grocery stores. Don't confuse mochi cakes with the sweets that are often called "mochi," which contain sugar. You want unflavored pounded rice cakes.)

A seven-herb congee for modern times, topped with mochi rice cakes

SERVES 2

¾ cup (150 g) uncooked short-grain rice
Small amounts of any combination of the
    following to total 2 cups (40 g):
    Daikon radish greens
    Baby turnip greens
    Arugula
    Parsley
    Watercress
    Mitsuba
    Mizuna greens
2¾ cups (700 ml) Kombu Dashi Stock (see
    page 12)
Salt, to taste
2 pieces mochi (glutinous rice cake)

1 Rinse the rice in several changes of water. Soak in enough water to cover for 15 minutes. Transfer to a fine-mesh sieve and allow to drain.

2 Chop all the greens and herbs coarsely.

3 Bring the kombu dashi stock to a boil in a saucepan over high heat. Add the rice and the salt. Cook according to the directions for Basic Congee on page 26. Broil the glutinous rice cakes in a toaster oven until they puff up and are lightly browned. Alternatively, dry-fry them over medium heat for 3 to 4 minutes per side.

4 Stir the green herbs and leaves into the congee and ladle into two bowls. Top each one with a piece of mochi.

ZEN VEGAN NOTE
You can buy ready-to-use seven-herb congee kits at a well-stocked Japanese grocery or any supermarket in Japan. Historically, however, this congee was made with whatever herbs and greens could be gathered in the wild, regardless of whether they were the designated types or seven in number. It's fine to be flexible and not adhere rigidly to tradition. Try making this with any kind of green herbs or greens.

Congee with Vegetables and Tofu

This colorful congee is full of interesting textures to enjoy: crunchy mushrooms, silky-smooth tofu, and tender carrot. If you can't find spring chrysanthemum greens, use arugula or other flavorful greens.

SERVES 2

Handful spring chrysanthemum greens, about 1 oz (30 g)
1 oz (30 g) enoki mushrooms
Piece of firm tofu, about 7 oz (200 g)
1 tablespoon sesame oil
¼ medium carrot, thinly sliced
¾ cup (185 ml) Kombu Dashi Stock (see page 12)
1 tablespoon miso paste
2 teaspoons cornstarch or potato starch dissolved in 2 to 3 teaspoons water
2 servings Basic Congee (see page 26)

1 Roughly chop the chrysanthemum greens. Remove the stem ends of the enoki mushrooms and cut into 1-inch (2.5 cm) pieces. Drain the tofu and cut into cubes.

2 Heat the sesame oil in a skillet. Add the greens, mushrooms and carrot and sauté over medium heat until wilted.

3 Add the drained tofu, dashi stock and miso. Cook for 2 more minutes, stirring frequently.

4 Add the cornstarch-and-water mixture and stir to thicken the sauce. (Add more if you want the sauce to be thicker.)

5 Ladle the congee into two bowls. Top each serving with plenty of tofu, vegetables and sauce.

The smooth miso-flavored sauce gently permeates the congee

ZEN VEGAN NOTE
This type of sauce, thickened with starch, is usually served with noodles, so serving it with congee may seem unusual—but it works very well. Cooking always reminds me of how limiting preconceptions and assumptions can be.

Bamboo Shoot Congee

The distinctive fragrance and flavor of the bamboo shoots permeates this congee, and makes it taste like spring. The crispy-crunchy texture enhances this. The green of the fava beans is so pretty too, don't you think?

This congee is filled with the umami of the bamboo shoots

SERVES 2

¾ cup (150 g) uncooked short-grain rice
Water for rinsing and soaking
4 oz (120 g) cooked bamboo shoots packed in water, well drained
18 pods fresh fava beans, shelled
2¾ cups (700 ml) Kombu Dashi Stock (see page 12)
½ tablespoon light soy sauce
½ tablespoon mirin
Salt, to taste

1 Rinse the rice in several changes of water. Soak in enough water to cover for 15 minutes. Transfer to a fine-mesh sieve and allow to drain.

2 Slice the bamboo shoots very thinly. Parboil the fava beans for 1 minute, then plunge in cold water. Drain well and remove skins.

3 Combine the kombu dashi stock, bamboo shoots soy sauce and mirin in a saucepan and bring to a boil over high heat. Add the rice and salt and cook according to the directions for Basic Congee on page 26.

4 Ladle the congee into two bowls and top with the shelled fava beans.

ZEN VEGAN NOTE
Slice the bamboo shoots as thinly as possible. Bamboo shoots are often cooked with rice, but they work very well in congee, too. Freshly dug bamboo shoots cooked with rice is a traditional harbinger of spring in Japan.

Saffron and Chestnut Congee

Saffron imparts a bright yellow color that is not only pretty to look at, but supplies vitamin B_1, which helps perk you up when you're feeling run down. The chestnut in this congee is reminiscent of a full moon floating in an autumn sky.

SERVES 2

2 whole peeled and cooked chestnuts
2 tablespoons dark soy sauce
2 tablespoons, plus 1¾ cups (425 ml) Kombu Dashi Stock (see page 12)
¾ cup (150 g) uncooked short-grain rice
Water for rinsing and soaking
Pinch of saffron threads
1¼ cups (300 ml) lukewarm water
½ red bell pepper
½ tablespoon light soy sauce
Salt, to taste

1 Marinate the chestnuts in the dark soy sauce and the 2 tablespoons kombu dashi for at least 4 hours. (You can use marrons glacés or chestnuts in syrup, but they must be soaked in plain water for 30 minutes before marinating to remove the sugar.)

2 Rinse the rice in several changes of water. Soak in enough water to cover for 15 minutes. Transfer to a fine-mesh sieve and allow to drain.

3 Soak the saffron threads in the lukewarm water. Slice the bell pepper thinly.

4 Combine the 1¾ cups kombu dashi stock, saffron with its soaking water, light soy sauce and bell pepper in a saucepan and bring to a boil over high heat. Add the rice and salt and cook according to the directions for Basic Congee on page 26.

5 Ladle the congee into two bowls, topping each one with a chestnut.

An elegant chestnut moon in your bowl

ZEN VEGAN NOTE
Otsukimi ("moon-viewing") is a fall festival on the 15th day of the eighth month of the old Japanese calendar, when people contemplated the full moon while wishing for a good harvest. The almost-full moon on the 13th day is called the Chestnut Moon, which was my inspiration for this congee.

Cucumber and Sesame Seed Congee

When you stir-fry summer-grown cucumbers, their flavor grows more expansive and intense. The crunchy texture tickles the taste buds and brings out the sweetness of the congee.

This congee is best made in summertime with cucumbers grown in the sun

SERVES 2

2 small Japanese or Asian cucumbers
2 tablespoons dark sesame oil
1-inch (2.5 cm) piece fresh ginger, finely shredded
1 tablespoon dark soy sauce
2 servings Basic Congee (see page 26)
Toasted black sesame seeds, to taste

1 Bash the cucumbers with a rolling pin or similar implement to bruise them, and then cut into bite-sized pieces.

2 Heat the sesame oil in a skillet and add the ginger. Sauté over low heat until the oil is fragrant. Turn the heat to high, add the cucumber quickly stir-fry them. When the cucumbers soften, add the soy sauce.

3 Ladle the congee into two bowls. Top each serving with cucumbers and sprinkle with sesame seeds.

ZEN VEGAN NOTE
The nutty sesame oil and the refreshing cucumber will help you overcome the summer heat. The key is to stir-fry the cucumbers quickly over very high heat.

Sweet Potato Congee

Reliable sweet potatoes keep for a long time and have sustained people during famines. I like to savor this congee while thinking back to the past with gratitude. If you can't find dried shiso seasoning (yukari), try sesame salt (see Step 1 of Sesame Salt Congee on page 27).

SERVES 2

¾ cup (150 g) uncooked short-grain rice
Water for rinsing and soaking
7 oz (200 g) sweet potato, preferably the
 purple-skinned Asian type
1 tablespoon dark sesame oil
Salt, to taste
3¼ cups (800 ml) Kombu Dashi Stock (see
 page 12)
Dried shiso seasoning (yukari), to taste

1 Rinse the rice in several changes of water. Soak in enough water to cover for 15 minutes. Transfer to a fine-mesh sieve and allow to drain.

2 Scrub the sweet potato, but do not peel. Cut into ½ inch (1.5 cm) cubes. Heat the sesame oil in a skillet, add the sweet potato, sprinkle with salt and sauté over medium heat until browned.

3 Bring the kombu dashi stock to a boil in a saucepan over high heat. Add the sweet potato and rice. Cook according to the directions for Basic Congee on page 26.

4 Ladle the congee into two bowls. Garnish with dried shiso or other seasoning.

Pan-fry the sweet potato to maximize its sweetness

ZEN VEGAN NOTE
Sweet potatoes were first grown in the Tokyo region in the 17th century by order of the eighth Tokugawa shogun, Yoshimune. He gave a man called Aoki Konyo the task of spreading the cultivation of sweet potatoes to save the people from famine.

Try this once and you'll be hooked

The stem is the tastiest part of the broccoli

Avocado and Shio Kombu Congee

Shio kombu is kombu seaweed cooked in a salty-sweet mixture of soy sauce and mirin and then dried. It can be found online and in Asian markets. Here it is combined with rich, buttery avocado, which is a good match for the salty shio kombu. Just use a little to top a bowl of plain congee, and you'll definitely keep coming back for more.

SERVES 2

1 avocado
⅓ oz (10 g) shio kombu seaweed
1 tablespoon dark sesame oil
Toasted white sesame seeds, to taste
2 servings Basic Congee (see page 26)

> **ZEN VEGAN NOTE**
> It is difficult to gauge exactly when an avocado is ripe. Sometimes you may cut one open and find it's started to turn black. No problem! A little discoloration is harmless. Accept the flaws in your produce with a big heart.

1 Peel the avocado and cut in half. Remove the pit, scoop out the flesh and chop finely. Put the avocado in a bowl with the shio kombu and sesame oil, and mix well.

2 Ladle congee into two bowls. Add the avocado mixture and sprinkle sesame seeds on top.

Ginger and Broccoli Congee

Cooked broccoli stems can be surprisingly sweet. Here they are diced and marinated with ginger in a soy and vinegar sauce, a perfect topping for plain congee.

SERVES 2

2 oz (50 g) broccoli stem
Piece of fresh ginger, about 1 oz (30 g)

For the marinade
3 tablespoons dark soy sauce
3 tablespoons rice vinegar
1 tablespoon sugar
1 small red chili pepper
2 servings Basic Congee (see page 26)

> **ZEN VEGAN NOTE**
> Even broccoli stems, which are often thrown away, can be enjoyed when prepared in the right way.

1 Peel the broccoli stem and ginger. Dice both into ¼-inch (5 mm) pieces.

2 Blanch the diced broccoli stem in boiling water for about 30 seconds.

3 Combine all marinade ingredients in a bowl and mix together. Add the diced broccoli and ginger. Marinate in the refrigerator overnight.

4 Ladle the congee into two bowls. Divide the marinade mixture between the bowls and serve.

Chapter 3

Zen Vegan
Main Dishes

Zen vegan cooking really lets vegetables shine.
When you serve a meal without any animal products, the flavors of
the vegetables take center stage and you may find dimensions to
these ingredients that you never tasted before. Enjoy!

Shiitake Mushrooms

These soft, round mushrooms not only look good, but they have great texture and absorb cooking juices like sponges. Try letting shiitake mushrooms sit in the sun for 30 minutes before cooking to intensify their umami. Shiitake Mushroom Dashi Stock (see page 12) plays a great supporting role in any dish with its unique hearty flavor. Save the stems of dried shiitake mushrooms for stock, or chop the fresh ones and use them along with the thick, meaty caps. Every part can be used!

The light tofu topping enhances the meaty mushroom caps

Simmered Tofu-stuffed Shiitake

The stuffing used here is a classic Japanese recipe called *shira-ae*, a thick tofu-based sauce with finely chopped vegetables. In addition to carrots and mitsuba leaves, the stems of shiitake mushrooms are included in this version. Juicy, umami-rich flavors fill every bite.

SERVES 2

Piece of silken tofu, about 7 oz
  (200 g)
6 large fresh shiitake mushrooms
¾ cup (200 ml) Kombu Dashi Stock
  (see page 12)
1 tablespoon light soy sauce
1 tablespoon mirin
1 tablespoon sake
¼ medium carrot, finely shredded
5 sprigs mitsuba, coarsely chopped
1 tablespoon sesame paste or tahini
1 teaspoon sugar
2 pinches salt, divided
½ tablespoon dark sesame oil

1 Drain the tofu. Wrap in a clean kitchen cloth or a double layer of paper towels and microwave on medium (500W) for 5 minutes. Alternately, place a plate on top and let stand for 30 minutes.

2 Remove the stems from the shiitake mushrooms. Discard the hard stem ends, slice the stems and set aside. Heat the kombu dashi stock, soy sauce, mirin and sake in a pan. Add the mushroom caps and simmer over medium heat for 5 minutes. Remove and allow to cool.

3 Blanch the carrot and mitsuba in boiling water for a few seconds. Drain well and squeeze out any excess moisture.

4 Put the drained tofu and blanched carrots and mitsuba in a bowl. Add the sesame paste, sugar and a pinch of salt and mix well.

5 Heat the sesame oil in a skillet over high heat. Add the sliced mushroom stems, sprinkle with a pinch of salt and sauté for a few minutes.

6 Add the mushroom stems and the sesame oil to the tofu mixture and stir well.

7 Place the simmered mushroom caps upside down on a serving plate and mound equal portions of the tofu mixture on each cap.

ZEN VEGAN NOTE
Don't discard the liquid you used to simmer the mushroom caps! It can be reserved for use in other simmered dishes or thinned with water to make a light soup.

Sweet corn brings out the umami in the mushroom stems

Corn and Shiitake Tempura

This type of tempura, where finely diced ingredients are mixed, coated with batter and fried, is called *kakiage*. The stems of shiitake mushrooms, which are often overlooked, are the stars here. Since each morsel is quite small, even people who aren't too fond of deep-fried foods will enjoy them. You can use canned or frozen corn kernels, but fresh corn is best for its intense sweetness.

SERVES 2

10 fresh shiitake mushrooms
½ ear fresh corn, or ¼ cup
   (40 g) corn kernels
5½ tablespoons cake flour
   or all-purpose flour,
   divided
¼ cup (65 ml) water
Vegetable oil, for frying
Salt, to taste

1 Cut the stems off the mushrooms and dice the caps. Discard the hard stem ends and slice the stems thinly. Use a knife to scrape the kernels off the corn cob.

2 Make the batter by combining 3½ tablespoons of the flour with the water. Mix briefly to blend.

3 Put the mushrooms and corn kernels in a separate bowl and dust with the remaining 2 tablespoons flour.

4 Heat the oil to 360°F (180°C). Stir the mushrooms and corn into the batter. Drop spoonfuls of the battered mushroom-and-corn mixture into the hot oil, 3 to 4 at a time. Deep-fry for 3 to 4 minutes or until just golden. Drain on a rack lined with paper towels.

5 Arrange on a serving plate and sprinkle with a little salt.

ZEN VEGAN NOTE
You may be discarding the stems from shiitake without thinking, but they are surprisingly tasty. If you have the time, try putting fresh shiitake in the sun for 30 minutes before cooking them. Their umami will become concentrated and really delicious! You can eat just about every bit of a mushroom.

Mixed Simmered Vegetables

This classic simmered dish is called *chikuzen-ni* in Japanese. It's usually made with chicken, but this is a vegan version. The ingredients are stir-fried with a generous amount of sesame oil for a rich, assertive flavor. Since each ingredient has different cooking times, the key is to pre-cook each one separately before combining them. If you don't have a microwave, steam the vegetables separately until just tender.

SERVES 2

6 dried shiitake mushrooms
Piece of konnyaku, about 10½ oz (300 g)
Piece of daikon radish, about 4 oz (120 g)
1 medium carrot
2 taro roots
2 tablespoons dark sesame oil
1 tablespoon sugar
Pinch of salt
1½ cups (375 ml) Kombu Dashi Stock (see page 12)
1 tablespoon mirin
3 tablespoons dark soy sauce
2 sprigs mitsuba, roughly chopped, for garnish

The sesame oil adds great depth and richness

1 Soak the dried shiitake overnight in enough water to cover. Drain, reserving the soaking water for stock if desired. Discard the stems and quarter the caps. Blanch the konnyaku in boiling water, then drain and cut into bite-sized pieces with a spoon.

2 Cut the daikon radish and carrot into chunks without peeling them. Put the pieces in a single layer in a microwave-safe dish, add 1 tablespoon of water and cover with cling film. Microwave on high (500W) for about 5 minutes.

3 Scrub the taro roots and microwave whole on high for 10 minutes. Peel while still hot.

4 Heat the sesame oil in a pan over medium heat. Add the shiitake mushrooms, daikon radish, carrot, taro, sugar and salt, and sauté over medium heat. When the vegetables begin to soften, add the dashi, mirin and soy sauce. Simmer over medium heat until the cooking liquid is almost gone.

5 Arrange in a serving bowl and top with the roughly chopped mitsuba.

ZEN VEGAN NOTE
Chikuzen-ni is considered a lucky dish, and is eaten as part of the New Year's feast. Each ingredient in the stew brings out the best qualities in the other ingredients harmoniously—much like a happy family or a smoothly running workplace.

Kombu Seaweed

In this section, we'll focus on ways to make use of the kombu seaweed that you used to make Kombu Dashi Stock (see page 12). This softened kombu, called *dashigara kombu*, has plenty of great flavor, even after some of its delicious umami has been imparted to the stock. Kombu seaweed is full of soluble and non-soluble fiber, minerals and other nutrients. Since it's already been softened in the dashi-cooking process, you can prepare it quite quickly by slicing it and simmering or frying to make delicious side dishes. Different kinds of seasonings make the kombu even tastier.

Kombu and umeboshi—a delicious combination

Kombu and Crispy Tofu with Umeboshi

The combination of the tender kombu seaweed, the rich abura-age deep-fried tofu and the salty-sour umeboshi pickled plums is surprisingly delicious. Quickly tossing the coating ingredients with the tofu while it's still hot allows the flavors to be absorbed better. The more slowly you savor this dish, the better it tastes.

SERVES 2

4 inch (10 cm) piece kombu left over from making Kombu Dashi Stock (see page 12)
1 umeboshi salt-pickled plum
2 tablespoons Kombu Dashi Stock (see page 12)
1 piece abura-age deep-fried tofu
1 teaspoon light soy sauce

1 Cut the kombu into very thin strips.

2 Pit the umeboshi and chop the pulp. Add the kombu dashi stock and mix together.

3 Dry-fry the abura-age in a skillet without any added oil until it is crispy on both sides. Cut into thin strips and sprinkle with the soy sauce while still hot.

4 Add the kombu strips and the umeboshi mixture to the tofu and toss to coat.

ZEN VEGAN NOTE
Salt-pickled umeboshi have been made in Japan for hundreds of years. During the Edo period (1603–1868), on New Year's Eve or the eve of an equinox, a tea called *fuku-cha* (good-luck tea) was made, from umeboshi, kombu, roasted black soybeans and sansho prickly ash berries. It was believed to help protect the drinker from harm.

A quick version of a Japanese classic with the zing of sansho pepper

Quick-simmered Kombu

Like the Seasoned Nori Seaweed on page 13, this recipe is based on a classic Japanese preserved dish called *tsukudani*. Here, bite-sized pieces of softened kombu are simmered in a combination of soy sauce and sugar. Since it's only cooked for a short time, the kombu retains its crunchy, chewy texture.

SERVES 2

2 tablespoons sugar
2 tablespoons dark soy sauce
2 tablespoons sake
4 tablespoons water
8 inch (20 cm) piece kombu left over
   from making Kombu Dashi Stock
   (see page 12)
Sansho pepper, to taste

1 Bring the sugar, soy sauce, sake and water to a boil in a pan over high heat. Allow to boil for a minute to cook off most of the alcohol.

2 Cut the kombu into bite-sized pieces. Add to the seasoning ingredients, reduce heat to low and simmer for about 10 minutes.

3 Turn off the heat and leave to cool in the liquid. Before serving, sprinkle with sansho pepper to taste.

ZEN VEGAN NOTE
Kombu *tsukudani* is available ready-made in Japanese grocery stores, but taking the time to make this everyday condiment yourself helps you truly appreciate it.

Crispy Fried Kombu

This simple dish just consists of kombu that is cut up and fried, but the results are amazingly good. The softened kombu gets nicely crisp on the outside, while the insides remain soft and tender. The oil really brings out the best in the kombu.

SERVES 2

8 inch (20 cm) piece kombu left over
    from making Kombu Dashi Stock
    (see page 12)
Bread flour or all-purpose flour, for
    dusting
Vegetable oil, for frying
Salt, to taste

1 Pat the kombu dry with paper towels and cut into pieces approximately 1 inch (2.5 cm) square. Dust with flour to coat.

2 Heat enough vegetable oil to cover the bottom of the skillet. Add the kombu and fry on both sides. The moisture in the kombu may cause the oil to spatter, so loosely cover the skillet with foil, leaving space for cooking chopsticks or cooking tongs. Hold the kombu pieces down as they cook, turning a few times.

3 When crisp, remove the kombu pieces from the oil and drain on layers of paper towel. Arrange on a serving plate and sprinkle with salt.

ZEN VEGAN NOTE
As mentioned above, the oil can spatter a lot because the softened kombu contains a lot of moisture. This can vary depending on the type of kombu you are using, however. It makes you realize just how many varieties of this seaweed there are.

Crispy on the outside, tender on the inside

Kabocha Squash

Kabocha squash has been enjoyed in Japan for centuries. It was believed that eating this nutritious hard-shelled squash on the winter solstice would prevent illness. The bright yellow-orange flesh is dense and sweet. Unlike many winter squashes, the delicate green peel can be eaten. Kabocha aligns perfectly with the Zen vegan principle of consuming the entire vegetable.

Vary the thickness of the peel for a range of textures and flavors

Deep-fried Kabocha Skins with Curry Salt

Deep-frying the peel of the kabocha squash really brings out its flavor. The spicy curry salt goes nicely with the sweetness of the kabocha squash flesh and the fragrance of the peel.

SERVES 2

Peel from ¼ kabocha squash
Cornstarch or potato starch, for dusting
Vegetable oil, for deep-frying
½ teaspoon curry powder
½ teaspoon salt

1 Cut the kabocha squash peel into bite-sized pieces and dust with the cornstarch.

2 Heat the vegetable oil to 340°F (170°C) and deep-fry the kabocha peel pieces for about 3 minutes. (If the pieces are thick, microwave them for a couple of minutes or steam briefly before frying them.)

3 Mix the curry powder and salt together. Serve on the side for dipping the fried kabocha squash pieces.

ZEN VEGAN NOTE
The texture of the kabocha squash peel will vary depending on how thick it is. Thin pieces will be crisp and savory, and thick ones will be dense and sweet. Try mixing both thick and thin pieces if you can, for variety.

Enjoy the striking green and orange colors of this dish

Doubled-up Kabocha Squash

In this dish, the green kabocha squash peel is blended into a sauce that complements the bright orange kabocha pieces. The kabocha is simmered in kombu dashi stock to subtly infuse it with umami. This is a great dish to serve with plain rice.

SERVES 2

¼ medium kabocha squash, pith and
  seeds removed, about 10½ oz
  (300 g)
3 tablespoons water, divided

A Seasonings
¾ cup (185 ml) Kombu Dashi Stock
  (see page 12)
½ tablespoon sugar
½ tablespoon light soy sauce
½ tablespoon mirin

B Seasonings
3 tablespoons Kombu Dashi Stock
½ tablespoon sesame paste or tahini
½ tablespoon light soy sauce

1 Peel the kabocha and set the peel aside. Cut the flesh of the squash into bite-sized pieces and place in a single layer on a microwave-safe plate. Sprinkle with 2 tablespoons water, cover with cling film and microwave on high (500W) for about 8 minutes, until soft.

2 Bring the A Seasonings to a boil in a saucepan. Add the kabocha from Step 1 and simmer for about 10 minutes over low heat.

3 Place the peel on a microwave-safe plate and add 1 tablespoon of water. Cover with cling film and microwave on the high setting for about 5 minutes.

4 Combine the B Seasonings and the kabocha peel and blend to a puree, leaving some texture.

5 Drain the simmered kabocha and transfer to a bowl. Pour the blended sauce over and toss to coat.

ZEN VEGAN NOTE
In Japanese cooking, a dish in which the main part and the "sauce" are made from the same ingredient is called *tomo-ae*, which means "mixed with itself." Recipes that use the entire vegetable, prepared with care, epitomize Zen vegan cooking.

Kabocha Squash Fritters with Almonds and Shiso

For these fritters, mashed kabocha is made into a dough, formed into dumplings and coated with almonds and green shiso leaves. To turn the kabocha dumplings into a dessert, serve them with sweet adzuki bean paste—a classic combination that is known as *toji* kabocha ("winter solstice kabocha") in Japanese. This sweet red bean paste (*koshi-an*) can be found at well-stocked Asian markets.

SERVES 2

¼ medium kabocha squash, pith and seeds removed
2 tablespoons water
5 green shiso leaves
6 tablespoons all-purpose flour, plus more for coating
Pinch of salt
1 tablespoon sliced almonds
Vegetable oil, for deep-frying
Smooth sweet red bean paste (optional)

1 Peel the kabocha. (Peel may be reserved for Deep-fried Kabocha Peel with Curry Salt on page 61.) Cut the flesh into small pieces and place in a single layer on a microwave-safe plate. Sprinkle with the 2 tablespoons water, cover with cling film and microwave on high (500W) for about 8 minutes, until soft. Cut each shiso leaf into 4 pieces.

2 Mash the cooked kabocha pieces in a bowl while still hot. Add the 6 tablespoons flour and salt and mix well. Divide and form into bite-sized patties.

3 Coat the patties lightly with flour. Press a piece of shiso leaf on one side and a few sliced almonds on the other side of each patty.

4 Heat the oil to 360°F (180°C) and deep-fry the patties until golden brown. Drain well. Serve with sweet red bean paste on the side. If you can't find red bean paste, you can also serve the fritters on their own, or with fruit jam.

ZEN VEGAN NOTE
The sweet kabocha squash, the fragrant shiso, and the crunchy almonds are all equal stars of this dish, while the red bean paste on the side adds a fourth dimension. This dish comes together because each ingredient has such unique characteristics.

A classic sweet and savory combination

Napa Cabbage

Napa cabbage (also called Chinese cabbage) is high in vitamins and minerals. Each part of the cabbage, from its outer leaves to its core, from its leaf tips to its stem ends, has a different texture and subtly differing flavors. It can be eaten raw, grilled, stir-fried, or stewed, making it a truly versatile vegetable with lots of dimensions to explore.

Tender leaf tips are perfect for salad

Napa Cabbage Salad with Nori Seaweed

The tender tips of the leaves of the napa cabbage are best eaten raw. With shredded nori seaweed, toasted sesame seeds and a dressing made with umami-rich light sesame oil, this Japanese-style salad is absolutely delicious.

SERVES 2

For the dressing
8 tablespoons light sesame oil
2 tablespoons dark soy sauce
4 tablespoons rice vinegar
Salt, to taste

Tips of 3–4 large napa cabbage outer leaves
1 small Japanese or Asian cucumber
Salt, to taste
½ sheet nori, torn into bite-sized pieces
Toasted white sesame seeds

1 Whisk dressing ingredients to blend.

2 Tear the leaf tips into bite sized pieces. Crisp in a bowl of cold water for about 5 minutes. Drain well.

3 Chop the cucumber finely. Place in a bowl with the napa cabbage leaf tips and the salt. Knead and squeeze lightly by hand until the leaves have wilted slightly. Pour the dressing over and toss to mix. Arrange on serving plates and top with the nori pieces and the sesame seeds.

ZEN VEGAN NOTE
Tearing the leaf tips into bite-sized pieces allows the dressing to coat them more fully. You'll enjoy this salad to the last drop of dressing.

Sauté the ingredients slowly and with care

Napa Cabbage Soup

The napa cabbage should be cooked slowly and thoroughly to bring out its maximum sweetness and tenderness. The umami of the sun-dried tomatoes adds depth and richness to this soul-satisfying soup.

SERVES 2

¼ large napa cabbage (cut lengthwise)
2–3 sun-dried tomatoes
1 tablespoon olive oil
Salt, to taste
2 cups (500 ml) Kombu Dashi Stock (see page 12)
1 tablespoon light soy sauce
2 teaspoons chopped parsley, for garnish

1 Remove the frilly leaf tips and inner leaves from the napa cabbage and reserve for another use. Slice the cabbage stems finely. Chop the sun-dried tomatoes.

2 Heat the olive oil in a saucepan. Add the napa cabbage and sprinkle with the salt. Sauté over low heat, stirring frequently, for about 10 minutes.

3 Add the tomatoes and the kombu dashi stock. Simmer over medium heat for about 5 minutes. Add the soy sauce and simmer for another minute. Garnish with chopped parsley.

ZEN VEGAN NOTE
The napa cabbage is stir-fried slowly over low heat; the more time you take, the more flavor you will be able to bring out. Cooking doesn't have to be difficult. To achieve great results, simply execute each step with attention and care.

Seared Napa Cabbage with Tomato Sauce

The key to this dish is to coat the leaves, especially the cut surfaces, with flour. The cabbage is seared so the outside becomes firm, while the insides of the stems will become very tender. The acidity of the fresh tomato sauce balances the flavors.

SERVES 2

¼ large napa cabbage (cut lengthwise)
All-purpose flour, for dusting
1 tablespoon light sesame oil

For the tomato sauce
½ medium tomato
3 sprigs parsley
1 tablespoon light sesame oil
Salt, to taste
1 tablespoon light soy sauce

1 Cut the napa cabbage quarter in half lengthwise and dust with flour. Heat the sesame oil in a skillet. Fry the napa cabbage over medium heat until it is golden brown on all sides.

2 To make the tomato sauce, dice the tomato finely and coarsely chop the parsley. Heat the sesame oil in a saucepan. Add the tomato and parsley and sprinkle with a little salt. Cook over high heat, stirring frequently, until the tomatoes have softened. Turn off the heat and add the soy sauce.

3 Arrange each piece of napa cabbage on a plate and top with tomato sauce.

ZEN VEGAN NOTE
Napa cabbage is often an accompaniment to a main dish, but here it takes center stage. It's such fun when an ingredient you've always left on the sidelines becomes a star player!

Seared napa cabbage is meltingly tender

Daikon Radish

The colder the season, the sweeter and more delicious daikon radish becomes. This root vegetable also helps keep our digestive systems healthy. The green leaves are a treasure trove of vitamins and minerals, and the outer peel of the roots has more vitamin C than the insides. This is one vegetable that really has to be eaten from top to tail, since each part is so tasty as well as nutritious.

Spicy Daikon Radish Peel

Kinpira is a classic Japanese stir-fried vegetable dish made with root vegetables. In this version, the peel of the daikon radish—which has a very different character from the flesh—is cut into fine matchsticks. It's so delicious, with such a wonderful crunchy texture, that you might be tempted to peel your daikon radish a little thicker so you get more of this dish.

SERVES 2

Peel of ½ large daikon radish
1 carrot, scrubbed but not peeled
1 small red chili pepper
2 tablespoons dark sesame oil
½ tablespoon sugar
½ teaspoon salt

Seasonings
⅓ cup (80 ml) Kombu Dashi Stock (see page 12)
1 tablespoon dark soy sauce
½ tablespoon mirin

1 Cut the daikon radish peel into thin matchsticks. Cut the carrot into similar thin matchsticks. Slice the chili pepper in half lengthwise and remove the calyx and seeds.

2 Heat the sesame oil in a skillet. Add the chili pepper and stir-fry over high heat for a few seconds. When the oil is fragrant, add the daikon peel and carrot. Add the sugar and salt and stir-fry until the vegetables are soft.

3 Add the seasonings to the pan and continue to stir-fry until the liquid has evaporated.

ZEN VEGAN NOTE
The name *kinpira* is said to come from a hero of a puppet theater play popular in the Edo period (1603–1868). The hero was a brave and undefeatable warrior called Kinpira Sakata. Perhaps eating a dish named after this hero will give you some of his courage!

The distinctive flavor and crunch of the daikon radish peel is addictive

All the flavors and textures of daikon radish in one dish

Daikon Radish Rice

A glazed, earthenware *donabe* pot is idea for this dish, since it heats up gradually. It really brings out the sweetness of the rice, making each grain plump and tasty. If you don't have a donabe, use a heavy cast-iron pot with a tight-fitting lid instead. Takuan pickles can be found at Japanese grocery stores.

SERVES 2

1½ cups (300 g) uncooked short-grain rice
⅛ large daikon radish

A Ingredients
1½ cups (300 ml) Kombu Dashi Stock (see page 12)
2 tablespoons light soy sauce
2 tablespoons mirin

B Ingredients
¼ serving Spicy Daikon Radish Peel (see page 69)
Marinated Daikon Radish Greens (see page 72), to taste
1½ oz (45 g) takuan (pickled daikon radish), quartered lengthwise and sliced thinly crosswise

1 Rinse the rice in several changes of water. Soak in clear water for 15 minutes, then drain in a fine-mesh sieve for about 15 minutes. Meanwhile, cut the daikon radish into matchsticks.

2 Combine the rice, the daikon radish and the A ingredients in an earthenware or cast-iron pot over medium-high heat. When the liquid comes to a boil, cover the pot, turn the heat down very low and steam-cook the rice for 12 minutes. Turn off the heat and leave the rice to cook with residual heat for 5 minutes.

3 Remove the lid and use a spatula to cut in the B ingredients, tossing gently to mix.

ZEN VEGAN NOTE
The entire daikon radish is used in this recipe—the leaves, the peel and the flesh. Each has a part to play, and leaving any of them out would make this dish incomplete.

Simmered Daikon Radish with Miso Sauce

Cooking the daikon radish in water saved from rinsing rice makes the root very tender. Cut the shiitake into fairly large pieces to enjoy the meaty texture.

SERVES 2

½ large daikon radish
Water saved from rinsing rice, for cooking daikon
1½ cups (375 ml) Kombu Dashi Stock (see page 12)
1 tablespoon light soy sauce
2 large fresh shiitake mushrooms
1 tablespoon dark sesame oil
1 tablespoon miso paste
2 tablespoons sake
1 tablespoon mirin

ZEN VEGAN NOTE
Steaming hot daikon with a miso and mushroom sauce is a satisfying and warming dish for a cold wintry day. Why not make extra andand invite a crowd over to enjoy it together?

1 Peel the daikon and slice into 2 inch (5 cm) thick rounds. (Reserve the peel for use in Spicy Daikon Radish Peel, page 69.) Arrange the daikon radish slices in a pan with enough rice rinsing water to cover. Bring to a boil over high heat.

2 When the liquid comes to a boil, reduce heat to low and slowly simmer the daikon radish until a wooden skewer pierces it easily. Once tender, drain the daikon in a colander and pat the surface dry with paper towels.

3 Combine the cooked daikon radish, kombu dashi stock and soy sauce in a saucepan and simmer over low heat for about 10 minutes.

4 Remove the stems from the shiitake mushrooms and roughly chop the caps. Discard the tough stem ends and slice the stems finely.

5 Heat the sesame oil in a small pan and add the mushroom caps and stems, miso, sake, and mirin. Simmer over low heat for about 2 minutes.

6 Ladle the daikon radish and cooking liquid into serving bowls. Top with the mushroom-miso sauce.

Savor the delicious flavor of slowly simmered daikon radish

Marinated Daikon Radish Greens

It is getting more difficult to buy daikon radish with the leafy tops intact these days, so if you come across any, make sure you snap them up! Here the nutrient-rich greens are chopped, and flavored with yuzu citrus juice. Use lime or lemon if you can't get hold of yuzu.

The sharp-tasting leaves cleanse the body

SERVES 2

3 oz (90 g) daikon radish greens
Peel of ½ yuzu citrus
⅓ teaspoon salt
1 tablespoon yuzu citrus juice
1 teaspoon light sesame oil

1 Chop the daikon radish leaves and yuzu peel finely.

2 Combine the leaves, peel, salt, yuzu juice and sesame oil in a bowl and mix well. Allow to marinate, covered, in the refrigerator overnight.

ZEN VEGAN NOTE
Daikon greens and yuzu go together beautifully. In the old days, yuzu was thought to keep away vengeful ghosts as well as guarding against catching a cold.

Chapter 4
Zen Vegan Italian Style

Even though they don't use "essential" Italian ingredients like cheese and garlic, these recipes are very Italian. Tofu does a lot of work by taking the place of cheese or ground meat, boosting the protein content of these dishes.

Four Creamy Soups

Make the most of vegetables that are in season

Suffused with intense mushroom flavor

Fresh corn makes this soup shine

Creamy Maitake Mushroom Soup

Maitake, meaning "dancing mushrooms" in Japanese, used to be so rare in the olden days that a person would dance with joy if they found some. This soup with its umami-rich mushrooms is so delicious that you may want to dance with joy too!

SERVES 2

7 oz (200 g) hen of the woods (maitake) or other mushrooms of your choice
1 tablespoon olive oil
Salt, to taste
Small piece silken tofu, about 2 oz (50 g)
1¾ cups (425 ml) Kombu Dashi Stock (see page 12)
1 tablespoon light soy sauce

1 Discard the tough stem ends of the mushrooms. Tear the mushrooms apart with your hands.

2 Heat the olive oil in a skillet. Add the mushrooms and a sprinkle of salt. Sauté slowly over medium-low heat until the mushrooms are soft. Remove from heat and allow to cool.

3 Combine the mushrooms, tofu and kombu dashi stock in a food processor or blender. Puree until smooth.

4 Transfer the mushroom puree to a pan and bring to a simmer over medium heat. Add the soy sauce before serving.

ZEN VEGAN NOTE
The key to preventing the mushrooms from getting burned is to cook them slowly over medium-low heat. This is an easy recipe, but you have to pay attention to the details.

Creamy Corn Soup

Creamy corn soup is very popular in Japan, but it's usually made with milk and butter. This Zen vegan version is best made when fresh corn is in season, so you can fully enjoy the natural sweetness of the corn. The smooth texture of the silken tofu makes it very creamy. If fresh corn is not available, use canned instead.

SERVES 2

½ ear fresh corn, or 3 oz (90 g) canned whole corn, including the liquid
Small piece silken tofu, about 2 oz (50 g)
1¾ cups (425 ml) Kombu Dashi Stock (see page 12)
Salt, to taste

1 Cook the ear of corn for 7 minutes in boiling water. Scrape the kernels and juice from the cob.

2 Combine the corn, tofu and kombu dashi stock in a food processor or blender, and puree until smooth.

3 Transfer to a pan and bring to a simmer over medium heat. Add salt to taste.

ZEN VEGAN NOTE
It is said that Christopher Columbus was astounded by the delicious flavor of sweet corn when he first ate it in the Americas. Corn, or maize, is said to have been cultivated since 3,000 BCE. Appreciating the history of the foods we cook is a way of paying respect.

The earthy flavors of this soup are deeply comforting

A very pretty light-green soup

Creamy Potato Soup

Umami-rich, filling potatoes are made creamy with silken tofu instead of milk or cream. This soup is very easy to eat. It's especially nice when you're feeling under the weather.

SERVES 2

1 medium potato, scrubbed but not peeled
1 tablespoon olive oil, plus additional oil for frying the peel
Salt, to taste
Small piece silken tofu, about 2 oz (50 g)
1¾ cup (425 ml) Kombu Dashi Stock (see page 12)

1 Remove the potato peel and reserve. Slice the flesh thinly.

2 Heat the olive oil in a skillet. Add the sliced potato, sprinkle with salt and stir-fry over medium heat until the potato is soft. Remove from heat and allow to cool.

3 Combine the potato, tofu and kombu dashi stock in a blender or food processor and puree until smooth.

4 Transfer the pureed potato to a pan and bring to a simmer over medium heat. Taste and adjust seasoning.

5 Heat additional olive oil in the skillet and fry the potato peel until crisp.

6 Top each bowl of soup with a piece of crispy peel.

ZEN VEGAN NOTE
Topping the soup with a crunchy strip of peel is both tasty and efficient. It feels great to eat a dish where no ingredient has gone to waste.

Creamy Edamame Soup

Edamame—fresh soybeans, picked when they are still green—have more flavor and fragrance than dried soybeans. It's worth taking the time to remove the thin membrane surrounding each bean. It dramatically improves the flavor and brightens the color.

SERVES 2

2½ oz (70 g) edamame in their pods
Small piece silken tofu, about 2 oz (50 g)
1¼ cups (300 ml) Kombu Dashi Stock (see page 12)
Salt, to taste

1 Bring a pot of water to a boil, put in the edamame pods and cook for 5 minutes. Shell when cool and peel the thin membrane off each bean.

2 Combine edamame, tofu and kombu dashi in a blender and puree until smooth.

3 Transfer to a pan and bring to a simmer over medium heat. Add salt to taste. This soup is also delicious cold.

ZEN VEGAN NOTE
During my training as a novice monk, I went through a ritual called the Worship of the 3,000 Buddhas. Every time I finished praying to a Buddha, I had to use chopsticks to transfer a dried soybean from one bowl to another without losing count. Removing the membranes from individual cooked edamame beans is hard work, too, but if you tackle them one at a time, you'll be done before you know it. Anything can be achieved if you take it step by step.

Vegetables and beans mingle harmoniously in this soup

Minestrone Soup

Even if a vegetable seems boring on its own, once several are combined together along with beans, the flavor becomes quite complex and interesting. Store-bought mixed beans will include several types with different colors and textures.

SERVES 2

¼ each yellow and red bell peppers
⅛ zucchini
¼ celery stalk
⅛ large cabbage
1 tablespoon olive oil
Salt, to taste
2 oz (50 g) canned mixed beans (or cooked beans of your choice)
⅔ cup (150 ml) Kombu Dashi Stock (see page 12)
⅔ cup (150 ml) Shiitake Mushroom Dashi Stock (see page 12)
¾ cup (185 ml) tomato juice
Minced parsley, to taste
Additional olive oil, to taste

1 Dice all the vegetables finely. Heat the olive oil in a saucepan, add the diced vegetables and sprinkle with salt. Cook, stirring, until the vegetables are tender.

2 Add the mixed beans, the kombu and shiitake dashi stock and the tomato juice. Bring to a boil.

3 Ladle into two bowls and top with minced parsley and a drizzle of olive oil.

ZEN VEGAN NOTE
The word minestrone in Italian simply means "soup." There are no rules—it's just a soup with many ingredients in it. Try making this with whatever vegetables you have on hand. The two kinds of dashi stock and the tomato juice will bring everything together in a delicious way.

Pan-fried Parsley

Whole parsley stalks are dusted with flour and pan fried—such a simple dish, but amazingly delicious. You'll think it's a waste to leave parsley uneaten on your plate after you've had this. With a squeeze of lemon, this is a perfect side dish to accompany an evening meal.

SERVES 2

6 whole parsley stalks
Bread flour or all-purpose flour, for dusting
1 tablespoon vegetable oil
Salt, to taste
¼ lemon, cut into two wedges

1 Dust the parsley with the flour.

2 Heat the oil in a skillet over high heat. Add the parsley and sprinkle with a little salt. Pan fry until crisp.

3 Arrange the fried parsley on plates with a wedge of lemon alongside.

ZEN VEGAN NOTE
I've always thought that parsley, which is usually relegated to being a garnish, should take center stage. It's one of the most nutritious dark green vegetables with plenty of iron and vitamins. Tuck into these crunchy bundles with gusto!

Parsley makes an excellent dish in its own right!

Pan-fried Green Peppers

Sear whole green peppers, rolling them around patiently, until they are charred on the outside. The insides get steam-cooked, seeds and all, and become meltingly tender. A drizzle of soy sauce finishes this dish.

SERVES 2

4 small green peppers
2 tablespoons dark sesame oil
1 tablespoon dark soy sauce

ZEN VEGAN NOTE
The seeds of the bell pepper are usually removed, but they actually have a pleasant texture and flavor. Looking at things differently often reveals a new perspective. Be sure to use very fresh peppers with plump white seeds.

1 Set a dry skillet over high heat until it is smoking hot. Add the whole peppers and sear them, turning frequently, until they are slightly charred and softened.

2 When the peppers are charred, add the sesame oil and fry for an additional 2 to 3 minutes.

3 Remove from heat and drizzle the soy sauce over.

A smoking hot pan brings out the flavor of the peppers

It looks like cheese, but it's not!

Zen Vegan Caprese Salad

At first glance it may look like cheese, but the white slices are actually tofu that's been marinated with kombu. In Zen vegan cooking, a limited number of ingredients are combined in creative ways. This dish really shows off the beauty of this approach.

SERVES 2

Piece of firm tofu, about 5 oz
   (150 grams)
Salt, to taste
Two 2 inch (5 cm) strips dried kombu
3 green shiso leaves
3 tablespoons olive oil
½ tablespoon miso paste
1 medium tomato
Toasted white sesame seeds, to taste

1 Drain the tofu thoroughly by wrapping it in several layers of paper towels and placing it in a colander or on a sieve. When drained, sprinkle with salt and sandwich between the kombu pieces. Place on a plate with a weight on top (such as another plate with a can on it) and refrigerate overnight.

2 Mince the shiso leaves finely and whisk together with the olive oil and miso and to make the pesto.

3 Pour off any liquid from the tofu and set the kombu aside. Slice the tofu thinly. Cut the tomato into rounds. Arrange the tomato slices on a serving plate and put tofu slices on top.

4 Cut the kombu used to marinate the tofu into very fine strips. Scatter over the tofu and tomato. Top each tofu slice with a dab of pesto. Garnish with sesame seeds.

ZEN VEGAN NOTE
I've used tofu to make a vegan "cheese" for this caprese. The kombu and the salt draw out moisture from the tofu to give it a cheese-like texture while adding lots of flavor. The kombu is also used for the garnish, for additional flavor and texture.

A refreshing lemony salad

Wakame Seaweed and Daikon Radish Salad

Wakame seaweed is a classic ingredient in Japanese-style salads. Fresh wakame seaweed packed in salt is available at well-stocked Japanese grocery stores. If you can't find it, substitute 2 tablespoons of dried wakame seaweed (available online), reconstituted in water.

SERVES 2

1 oz (30 g) fresh wakame
  seaweed packed in salt
Piece of daikon radish, about 5 oz
  (150 g)
1 medium tomato
Pinch of lemon zest
Salt, to taste

For the dressing
2 tablespoons freshly squeezed
  lemon juice
Pinch of lemon zest
¼ cup (65 ml) olive oil
Salt, to taste

1 Rinse the wakame seaweed in several changes of water to remove the salt, and cut into bite-sized pieces. Shave the daikon radish into thin strips with a peeler. Combine with the wakame and mix and massage by hand. Cut the tomato into bite-sized pieces and toss with the wakame and daikon radish.

2 Combine the dressing ingredients in a separate bowl and whisk until the salt has dissolved.

3 Arrange the salad in two bowls and pour the dressing over. Toss lightly and sprinkle with lemon zest and salt to taste.

ZEN VEGAN NOTE
Before juicing a lemon, be sure to remove the zest from the rind. In this recipe, grate or finely mince the zest to sprinkle on top of the salad. Freeze any leftover zest for use in other dishes.

Kombu seaweed performs double duty in this dish

Carpaccio of Turnips and Carrots

A traditional carpaccio is made with thin slices of fish or meat marinated in olive oil and other seasonings. In this "Zen vegan Italian" version, turnip and carrot slices infused with kombu are served with a sauce made of turnip greens. Note that this dish should be started the day before serving.

SERVES 2

2 small Asian turnips or baby turnips, with greens
1 medium carrot
Salt, for sprinkling, plus more to taste
3 inch (7 cm) long piece dried kombu
¼ cup (65 ml) Kombu Dashi Stock (see page 12)
2 tablespoons olive oil

1 Peel the turnips, reserving the peel and greens. Peel the carrot. Slice peeled turnips and carrot thinly. Sprinkle with salt, then layer the slices and the kombu in a container. Cover and refrigerate overnight to marinate. The salt will draw out their moisture, which will soften the kombu, and the umami from the kombu will permeate the vegetables.

2 Bring a saucepan of water to a boil. Add the turnip peel, boil for a couple of minutes, then add the turnip greens and boil for another minute or two. Drain and let cool. Put both the peel and greens into a food processor or blender with the kombu dashi stock and a little salt. Puree until smooth.

3 Arrange the turnip and carrot slices on a serving plate and pour the sauce over them, then drizzle with the olive oil. Thinly sliver the kombu used to marinate the vegetables and scatter across the plate.

ZEN VEGAN NOTE
The kombu used to marinate the vegetables is reserved to garnish the finished dish. When softened, the kombu becomes a little sticky and very tasty. There's a saying in Japanese that leftovers bring good fortune, and I think that applies to this dish. Try varying the vegetables—for example, daikon and cucumbers also work well.

An Italian-style version of a classic Japanese dish

Marinated Eggplant

This is an Italian-flavored take on the classic Japanese dish *nasu agebitashi* featuring deep-fried and marinated eggplant. The skin and insides of the eggplant are cooked in different ways, so you can enjoy two textures from one vegetable. Start this dish a day in advance so the eggplant has time to marinate.

SERVES 2

2–3 small Japanese or Asian eggplants
Oil, for deep-frying

A Marinade
¾ cup (185 ml) Kombu Dashi Stock
**   (see page 12)**
2 tablespoons light soy sauce
4 tablespoons sugar
1 small red chili pepper

B Marinade
1 slice fresh ginger
1 tablespoon olive oil
Pinch of salt

Minced parsley, for garnish
Balsamic vinegar, for garnish

1 Peel the eggplants, reserving the peel. Heat the oil to 360°F (180°C) and deep-fry the eggplants until tender. Drain well and combine with the A marinade ingredients. Marinate overnight.

2 Whisk together the ingredients for the B marinade. Add the uncooked peel pieces and marinate overnight.

3 Arrange the marinated eggplant and peel on a sharing plate. Garnish with minced parsley and a splash of balsamic vinegar.

ZEN VEGAN NOTE
Preparing the insides and the skin of the eggplant differently produces two very different textures and flavors. Although the skin is slightly bitter, it contains health-giving polyphenols—which brings to mind the old saying, "good and bad are two sides of the same coin."

The photogenic presentation adds to the enjoyment

Grilled Baby Turnips with Mustard-Olive Sauce

When turnips are cooked slowly, they turn meltingly soft and sweet. In this recipe, simmered baby turnips are seared on the surface with olive oil and served with a flavorful mustard sauce.

SERVES 2

2 baby turnips
Greens from 1 turnip
½ medium tomato
2 pitted black olives
1½ tablespoons grainy mustard
2 tablespoons olive oil, plus more for frying
Salt, to taste

1 Bring a pan of water to a boil. Add the whole turnips and simmer over low heat until a skewer pierces them easily. Drain and cut the turnips in half.

2 Finely chop the turnip greens and tomato. Roughly chop the olives. Combine greens, tomato and olives in a bowl. Add the mustard and the 2 tablespoons of olive oil and mix well.

3 Heat additional olive oil in a skillet. Add the cooked turnips, sprinkle with salt, and fry until browned.

4 Arrange the turnip halves on a serving plate. Spoon some sauce on each one.

The flavors of land and sea come together in this one-dish recipe

Mushroom and Nori Seaweed Risotto

Mushrooms, which are gathered from the land, are stir-fried thoroughly to maximize their flavor. The rice is infused with umami, and the nori, which comes from the sea, is added at the last moment for even more taste and fragrance. Miso, a fermented food that epitomizes Japanese cuisine, brings land and sea together.

SERVES 2

3½ oz (100 g) enoki mushrooms
3½ oz (100 g) hen of the woods (maitake) mushrooms
¼ celery stalk
2 tablespoons olive oil, divided
Salt, to taste
¾ cup (150 g) uncooked white short-grain rice or Italian risotto rice such as arborio
2 cups (500 ml) Kombu Dashi Stock (see page 12)
1 whole sheet nori seaweed
½ tablespoon miso paste
Minced parsley, for garnish

ZEN VEGAN NOTE
Risotto is cooked patiently and slowly, and you shouldn't mess around with it too much either. It's just like getting along with other people, or bringing up children, isn't it?

1 Chop the mushrooms and celery finely.

2 Heat 1 tablespoon of olive oil in a skillet and add the mushrooms and celery. Sprinkle with salt and sauté over medium heat until everything is wilted. Transfer to a plate.

3 Heat the remaining tablespoon of olive oil in the skillet and add the rice. Sauté over low heat until translucent. Return the mushrooms and celery to the skillet and sauté for a couple of minutes.

4 Heat the kombu dashi and add it to the skillet a little at a time, stirring after each addition. Continue to cook, stirring periodically, until the rice is tender.

5 Tear the nori into small pieces and add to the risotto. Just as the rice is cooked, stir in the miso. Turn off the heat after the miso is added, or it will rapidly lose its flavor. Garnish with parsley.

Hearty and satisfying, yet lower in calories than its meaty counterpart

Spaghetti with "Meat" Sauce

This has a "meat" sauce without any meat, but it's still very substantial and satisfying. This is a really handy sauce to have in your vegan repertoire.

SERVES 2

4 oz (120 g) uncooked spaghetti
Piece of firm tofu, about 7 oz (200 g)
2 tablespoons olive oil, divided, plus more for serving
3 fresh shiitake mushrooms
½ celery stalk
1 small bell pepper or ½ large bell pepper
¼ medium carrot
Salt, to taste
3½ oz (100 g) canned diced tomatoes
¾ cup (185 ml) Kombu Dashi Stock (see page 12)
1½ tablespoons miso paste
Chopped parsley, to taste

1 Cook the spaghetti, following the directions on the packet.

2 Drain the tofu in a colander for a few minutes. Heat 1 tablespoon of the olive oil in a skillet and crumble in the tofu. Sauté over high heat until the water has evaporated. Transfer to a bowl and set aside.

3 Discard the stem ends from the shiitake and coarsely chop the rest. Slice the celery stalk thinly crosswise. Discard the calyx from the pepper and dice the remainder, seeds and all. Quarter the carrot lengthwise and slice thinly crosswise.

4 Heat the second tablespoon of olive oil in the skillet and add the vegetables. Sprinkle with a little salt. Sauté over medium heat until vegetables are tender.

5 Add the canned tomatoes and kombu dashi stock to the pan. Simmer over medium heat for about 3 minutes.

6 Remove from heat. Add the miso to the pan and stir well. Add add salt to taste. Mix the sauce with the cooked spaghetti. Sprinkle with chopped parsley and drizzle with a little olive oil to serve.

ZEN VEGAN NOTE
The tofu, sautéed to remove moisture, takes the place of meat in this recipe. The shiitake mushrooms also have a meaty texture. The texture of the pepper seeds further enhances this dish.

Sauté the tofu quickly over high heat and avoid moving the skillet around, so that the moisture evaporates thoroughly and the texture becomes crumbly, like ground meat.

Tomato and Avocado Pasta

The richness of the avocado and the umami of the tomato work together to make a dish that is just as delicious as traditional Italian dishes. Miso is the indispensable ingredient that brings it all together.

Miso works really well in Italian-style dishes.
Buon appetito!

SERVES 2

4 oz (120 g) uncooked capellini or angel-hair pasta
1 large tomato
1 tablespoon miso paste
1 large avocado
2 tablespoons olive oil, plus more for serving
Additional olive oil, to taste

1 Cook the capellini according to the directions on the packet. Drain, then plunge into cold water immediately to maintain firmness. Drain well.

2 Chop the tomato coarsely. Add the miso paste and continue chopping the tomato, incorporating the miso as you go.

3 Peel and pit the avocado. Chop finely.

4 Combine the tomato and avocado in a bowl, add the olive oil and mix well.

5 Mix the tomato and avocado with the pasta. Arrange on plates and drizzle with additional olive oil.

After chopping the tomato coarsely, put the miso on top and continue mincing the tomato, mixing the miso paste in as you work.

ZEN VEGAN NOTE
I find it rather humorous that a priest like me, who has a distant relationship with hair, is cooking with angel-hair pasta! You can also use somen noodles for this dish, or any thin wheat noodle.

Spaghetti with Green Vegetable Pesto

Combining komatsuna greens, miso, sesame paste and olive oil makes for a fabulous quick and easy pasta sauce. Other leafy green vegetables such as chrysanthemum greens, spinach or chard work equally well in this dish.

SERVES 2

4 oz (120 g) uncooked spaghetti
Large bunch komatsuna greens, about 10½ oz (300 g), or other dark green leafy vegetable
3 large fresh shiitake mushrooms
1 tablespoon miso paste
1 tablespoon sesame paste or tahini
2 tablespoons olive oil, divided
Salt, to taste
Toasted white sesame seeds, for garnish

1 Cook the spaghetti according to the directions on the packet.

2 Bring a pot of water to a boil. Blanch the komatsuna greens for 1 to 2 minutes. Drain well, reserving some of the cooking liquid. Discard the hard stem ends of the shiitake mushrooms. Cut the stems into quarters and slice the caps thickly.

3 Combine the blanched komatsuna greens, miso, sesame paste, 1 tablespoon of the olive oil and 3 tablespoons of the reserved cooking liquid from the greens in a food processor or blender. Puree until smooth.

4 Heat the remaining 1 tablespoon olive oil in a skillet. Add the shiitake mushrooms, sprinkle with salt and sauté over medium heat.

5 Add the cooked spaghetti to the skillet and toss well to mix.

6 Take the pan off the heat. Stir in the pureed greens. Taste and add salt if necessary. Sprinkle sesame seeds on top to serve.

ZEN VEGAN NOTE
Miso and sesame paste are essential to Zen vegan food. Here they are used to add richness and umami in lieu of cheese.

Shiitake mushrooms have a meat-like texture and richness

Light and creamy cutlets

Milan-style "Cutlets"

Fried in plenty of olive oil and topped with a tangy dressing, these vegan cutlets are just as hearty and satisfying as the meaty kind.

SERVES 2

5 oz (150 g) Chinese yam or yamato yam, or 3 tablespoons
   tapioca flour mixed with 1 tablespoon water to form a paste
Piece of firm tofu, about 7 oz (200 g)
1 tablespoon minced parsley
2 tablespoons bread flour or all-purpose flour
½ teaspoon salt

For the dressing
¼ cup (65 ml) olive oil
½ teaspoon salt
2 tablespoons lemon juice
1 medium tomato, cut in bite-sized pieces
2 long sprigs fresh basil (leaves and stems), torn into pieces
1 sprig watercress, torn roughly (optional)

Olive oil, for cooking
2 small lemon wedges

1 Grate the yam without peeling. Drain the tofu well and crumble into a bowl.

2 Add the grated yam or tapioca flour paste, the parsley, the 2 tablespoons of flour and the ½ teaspoon of salt to the tofu. Knead thoroughly by hand.

3 To make the dressing, whisk together the olive oil, salt and lemon juice in a separate bowl. Stir in the tomato, basil and watercress and mix to incorporate.

4 Heat a generous amount of olive oil in a skillet. Form the tofu mixture into 2 large patties. Pan-fry over medium heat until golden brown on both sides.

5 Transfer the patties to two plates. Pour the dressing over and serve with a lemon wedge on the side.

ZEN VEGAN NOTE
This recipe represents the category of Zen vegan cooking called *modoki*, dishes that resemble the look, taste and texture of classic dishes that usually contain animal proteins. Part of the enjoyment lies in forgetting our preconceptions about how food "should" be, and just taking things in as they are.

Kneading the tofu and the Chinese yam thoroughly by hand gives the "cutlets" a soft, fluffy yet creamy texture.

Afterword

There is a teaching in Buddhism that says, "Mountains, rivers, grasses and trees are all Buddha." Life is present not only in animals, but in mountains, rivers and all kinds of plants, and all existence is dependent on the support of every other life.

On a typical day, my dinner might consist of white rice, miso soup with eggplant and tofu, stewed kabocha squash and cucumbers pickled in rice bran. You might think of this as just a vegan meal if you ate it at home. But if you ate it at a temple, you would probably consider it to be *shojin ryori*, or Buddhist temple cuisine. The difference is clear: it is only really Buddhist vegan cuisine if both the person cooking the meal and the one eating the meal think of it as such . For me personally, it's not so much whether the food is of animal or vegetable origin, it's more about believing that we shouldn't take what we eat for granted—we must realize that sitting down to eat a meal is a blessed act worthy of gratitude.

I would like to offer my sincere thanks to all the people who were involved in the publication of this book. I would also like to express my appreciation for my family, the parishioners of my temple, the people of our local community, the people who have participated in our cooking gatherings and meditation sessions, my elders at the temple, my friends and countless other people. I extend my sincerest gratitude to you all.

My hope is that, through trying out the recipes in this book, you may feel just a bit closer to the endless depths of Buddhism.

Gassho,
Koyu Iinuma

Index

"Books to Span the East and West"

Tuttle Publishing was founded in 1832 in the small New England town of Rutland, Vermont [USA]. Our core values remain as strong today as they were then—to publish best-in-class books which bring people together one page at a time. In 1948, we established a publishing office in Japan—and Tuttle is now a leader in publishing English-language books about the arts, languages and cultures of Asia. The world has become a much smaller place today and Asia's economic and cultural influence has grown. Yet the need for meaningful dialogue and information about this diverse region has never been greater. Over the past seven decades, Tuttle has published thousands of books on subjects ranging from martial arts and paper crafts to language learning and literature—and our talented authors, illustrators, designers and photographers have won many prestigious awards. We welcome you to explore the wealth of information available on Asia at **www.tuttlepublishing.com**.

Published by Tuttle Publishing, an imprint of Periplus Editions (HK) Ltd.

www.tuttlepublishing.com

KANTAN! OTERA GOHAN
Copyright © 2017 Koyu Iinuma
English translation rights arranged with
TOKUMA SHOTEN PUBLISHING CO., LTD.
through Japan UNI Agency, Inc., Tokyo

English translation by Makiko Itoh. English translation copyright © 2021 Periplus Editions (HK) Ltd.

ISBN: 978-4-8053-1661-0

Distributed by

North America, Latin America & Europe
Tuttle Publishing
364 Innovation Drive
North Clarendon, VT 05759-9436 U.S.A.
Tel: 1 (802) 773-8930
Fax: 1 (802) 773-6993
info@tuttlepublishing.com
www.tuttlepublishing.com

Japan
Tuttle Publishing
Yaekari Building 3rd Floor
5-4-12 Osaki
Shinagawa-ku
Tokyo 141-0032
Tel: (81) 3 5437-0171
Fax: (81) 3 5437-0755
sales@tuttle.co.jp
www.tuttle.co.jp

Asia Pacific
Berkeley Books Pte. Ltd.
3 Kallang Sector #04-01
Singapore 349278
Tel: (65) 6741 2178
Fax: (65) 6741 2179
inquiries@periplus.com.sg
www.tuttlepublishing.com

24 23 22 21
10 9 8 7 6 5 4 3 2 1

Printed in Malaysia   2106TO